THE

BEGINNER'S

GUIDE TO

ZEN

BUDDHISM

THE

BEGINNER'S

GUIDE TO

ZEN

BUDDHISM

JEAN SMITH

BELL TOWER NEW YORK

Grateful acknowledgment is made for use of the following:
Illustrations: Archives of Zen Mountain Monastery, pages 26, 34, 37, 39, 45,
46 (right), 48, 52, 53, 54, 55, 59, 61, 71, 161;
Elizabeth Grace Burkhart, pages 14, 15, 18, 50, 152;
Jisho Warner, pages 40 (top, bottom), 98,
and *Oxherding Picture #4, Catching the Ox,* page 130;
Thomas Hakanson, page 40 (middle).
All other photographs are by the author.
Text: Excerpts on pages 139, 140, 141 from *Plum Village Chanting
and Recitation Book* (1999) by Thich Nhat Hanh,
reprinted by permission of Parallax Press, Berkeley, California;
excerpts on pages 120, 121, 136 reprinted by permission
of the Zen Peacemaker Order; excerpts on pages 132–133, 138, 139 reprinted
by permission of the Zen Center of Los Angeles; excerpt on page 137
reprinted by permission of the Community of Mindfulness/NY Metro;
excerpt on pages 114–115 reprinted by permission of Nancy Mujo Baker.

Published by Bell Tower, New York, New York.
Member of the Crown Publishing Group.

Random House, Inc. New York, Toronto, London, Sydney, Auckland
www.randomhouse.com

Bell Tower and colophon are registered trademarks
of Random House, Inc.

Printed in the United States of America
Design by Barbara Sturman

Library of Congress Cataloging-in-Publication Data
Smith, Jean.
The beginner's guide to Zen Buddhism / Jean Smith.
Includes bibliographical references and index.
1. Zen Buddhism.   2. Spiritual life—Zen Buddhism.   I. Title.
BQ9265.4.S53   1999
294.3'927—dc21   99–35110
CIP
ISBN 0-609-80466-9

10 9 8 7 6

To those who teach us that

we are already whole

CONTENTS

Preface

You can't practice Zen Buddhism by reading a book.

BUT IF YOU ARE JUST beginning to look into meditation practice and Zen Buddhism, you may find yourself confronted by such an array of unfamiliar—and perhaps even contradictory—suggestions and ideas that you don't know even where to start. So you don't.

It you're stymied by how to begin, *The Beginner's Guide to Zen Buddhism* is intended for you. This is not a "dharma book" that expounds the teachings of Zen Buddhism. Rather, it's a brief collection of signposts to get you started. Although you can't develop a meditation practice through reading, any more than you can master a new city by looking at a map, you *can* orient yourself to the direction you want to take in your exploration. Let this book be your first guide as you begin what may well be the quest —and the most challenging adventure— of your life.

The inspiration for much of the material in this guide is the teachings of Pat Enkyo O'Hara Sensei, resident teacher of the Village Zendo in New York City, to whom I am greatly appreciative, but the emphasis and expression of everything within this book are entirely my own responsibility. *Gassho*, Enkyo.

Introduction

FINDING WHAT

YOU'RE SEEKING

There's a ragged uneasiness around the edges of your awareness. You realize instinctively that something is missing in your life. You try to fill that space with television and consumption, but you've discovered that they don't really satisfy you. It's like an itch that can't be scratched—something you can't quite reach even through psychotherapy or martial arts or a self-help group. You need something that gives you a deeper draught, a more fulfilling sense of understanding.

THE AWARENESS THAT something is missing in life is generally what motivates people to explore Zen Buddhism. As we try to learn how to fill the emptiness, meditation—zazen—is our greatest teacher. When we sit—even if our first experience is five minutes of a buzzing mind and a twitching body—we can begin to see something about the nature of our mind, and we discover that we want to find out more. Meditation allows the

The shape of the window at this Japanese-style zendo is derived from the head of a flame.

mind to stop getting caught up in the attachments that are insatiable. Meditation enables us to practice Zen Buddhism. But just what *is* Zen?

THE SEARCH FOR "ZEN"

We can talk about Buddhism and about Zen Buddhism from many different perspectives—religion, philosophy, psychology, art. But perhaps the best way to see Zen is as a way of life.

Certainly Zen can be practiced as a religion, but it doesn't have to be. In fact, many of us in the West came to Zen because we wanted to get away from religion. Then we discovered that there are many aspects of Zen—formal elements, services, rituals—that look very much like religion. Religion is a tricky concept. From one perspective, it can be seen as obscuring insight by force-feeding adherents what they are supposed to believe. But religion can also be seen as something that nourishes insight and allows it to be passed on. That's the sense in which the word *religion* applies to Zen: Zen provides a structure that supports our exploring the practice and the teachings for ourselves. Philosophy implies a way of thinking about, a point of view about, the world. Psychology emphasizes a way of understanding how people respond to life. Zen Buddhism has all of these elements of religion, philosophy, and psychology, but seeing Zen as a *way of life* brings practice down to day-in and day-out, everyday living.

Vietnamese Zen master Thich Nhat Hanh, in *Zen Keys,* captured the everyday nature of Zen practice when he recalled a conversation between the Buddha and a renowned philosopher:

"I have heard that Buddhism is a doctrine of enlightenment. What is your method? What do you practice every day?"

"We walk, we eat, we wash ourselves, we sit down."

"What is so special about that? Everyone walks, eats, washes, sits down. . . ."

"Sir, when we walk, we are aware that we are walking; when we eat, we are aware that we are eating. . . . When others walk, eat, wash, or sit down, they are generally not aware of what they are doing."

In Buddhism, mindfulness is the key. Mindfulness is the energy that sheds light on all things and all activities, producing the power of concentration, bringing forth deep insight and awakening. Mindfulness is at the base of all Buddhist practice.

An ancient koan, or teaching story, likens entering into genuine Zen practice as stepping forward from the top of a hundred-foot pole. How do people take this first step? What does it feel like? To a certain extent, the answers depend upon who you are and where you are and when you decide to step off the top of the pole.

One generation of American Buddhists stepped off by reading the Japanese Buddhist scholar D. T. Suzuki in high school in the 1950s and 1960s, then moved on to books by Alan Watts, Jack Kerouac, and the beatnik "dharma bums." For many of these people, some of the ideas from Japan, especially the notions of aesthetic freedom within certain formal constraints, initially had great appeal. This interest was primarily Buddhism *from the neck up,* based on books. In those days, a book on Zen came out only once every several years, so people could read everything that was published. But reading alone consistently proved unsatisfactory, and they eventually went in search of the practice itself.

In the half-century since then, the interest in Buddhism and especially Zen Buddhism has grown and has spread. There are many more books, but there are also myriad other expressions of and resources for encouraging that first step off the pole. Even in relatively small cities, at Zen centers or local colleges, you usually can find courses in *ikebana,* Japanese flower arrangement, within the framework of Zen; in *haiku,* the Japanese poetry form that expresses the nonduality of Zen; and certainly in *zazen,* meditation.

Today many people start out as "Zennists" rather than as Buddhists. They embrace some of the wonderful aspects of Zen—the aesthetic, especially the Japanese style, as well as the freedom, swashbuckling wit, and great spirit of humor and rebellion. They meditate and feel that their practice is complete without ever realizing that it rests on the larger foundation of the old teachings of Buddhism. But the longer they practice, the more they come to see that what first attracted them were the artifacts of a tradition. The living, breathing element of Zen—what is underneath it—comes out of the Four Noble Truths, which are explored in chapter 6 and are quintessentially what the Buddha saw. Today, the life and teachings of the Buddha—through the ecumenism that marks American Buddhism—have become integral to practice.

Many different types of Buddhism are currently being practiced in the United States. The three forms of Buddhism that the most Americans embrace today—all based on the Buddha's teachings but having different emphases—are Zen, in its Soto and Rinzai schools; Tibetan, or Himalayan; and Vipassana, or Insight Meditation. Although we shall look more closely at the history of Zen in chapter 5, we can just say here that the Mahayana ("Great Vehicle") tradition encompasses both Zen and Tibetan Buddhism and stresses seeking enlightenment for all beings. The oldest tradition, Theravada Buddhism (the "teachings of the elders"), sometimes disparagingly called Hinayana ("Lesser Vehicle"), primarily exists here as Vipassana, or Insight Meditation, and stresses the enlightenment of the individual for the benefit of all beings. Ultimately, you need a practice of some kind, and what distinguishes Vipassana or Tibetan practice from Zen practice is the form—the meeting place, the rituals, the manner of teaching, the lengths of sitting periods, and the meditation styles. Although meditation has the same goal in all traditions, each practice has quite distinctive characteristics.

WHY CHOOSE ZEN?

It's very important to find the tradition and the center where you are comfortable. The aspect of Zen that appeals to most people is its emphasis on zazen and the experience of meditating in a zendo, which we'll investigate in chapters 2 and 3. The word *Zen* comes from the Sanskrit *dhyana* ("meditative absorption"), which was transliterated into *ch'an* in Chinese, then into *zenna*, or *Zen*, in Japanese. The practice has come to this country as Zen; *zazen* literally means "seated mind."

Another attraction has to do with Zen teachers, discussed in chapter 4. Zen Buddhism emphasizes a strong, ongoing relationship between a student and a teacher. When you work with a Zen teacher, you're not just in a room with a hundred other students, but you have the opportunity to meet one-on-one with a teacher. And a quite wonderful aspect of Zen teachers is the freshness, the broad sense of humor, and the unpredictably bizarre methods they sometimes use to teach. The rhetoric of Zen, like that of all traditions, promises freedom. But Zen's reputation for being especially free goes back to irreverent, rebellious kinds of "crazy masters" found throughout Zen history. For this reason, *spontaneity* is a good word for the accepted norms of teaching and learning in Zen.

A special characteristic of Zen is a kind of intimacy with what you see and hear, which leads to a practice distinguished by its simplicity. When you meditate deeply, you become acutely mindful of just what surrounds you, and you develop a keen awareness of its aesthetics. Zen has been criticized as being excessively formal, but the teachings themselves are *right* within that form. People often have a moving experience arising out of their familiarity with form: Coming into a zendo—

where all the cushions are lined up, everything is spotless, everything has a particular place, and you bow in a particular way—is like being enfolded in a safe and still container. It may seem paradoxical that this intimacy with form occurs within the same context as crazy teaching. But they go together, because without that form the wild teaching wouldn't be so wild.

Finally, although storytelling is also part of the teaching approach within the Tibetan and Vipassana traditions, what sets Zen apart is koans, story-riddles whose every answer seems to be paradoxical, examined in chapter 2.

THE BENEFITS OF PRACTICE

When you first begin to meditate —in any tradition— you suddenly become awestruck by all the things going on in your mind. With practice, an incredible empowerment takes place as you begin to recognize and even to stop the constant chatter of thought. During the early months, you may experience this awareness of and ability to have some control over your thoughts as a honeymoon period.

After you've been practicing longer, perhaps during a retreat, all your ideas—the rigidities—about practice abruptly drop away, and you first *experience* intimacy with form. In this remarkable transformation, you recognize not just the form of Zen but also the form of your life. It's as if you suddenly can affirm, "Yes, *this* is my life."

Many advantages of Zen often are ballyhooed in the media under the all-inclusive term *stress reduction*. American Zen teacher Charlotte Joko Beck, in *Everyday Zen*, has succinctly deflated such notions. She insists that practice is not about producing psychological or physical change or bliss states, not about knowing the nature of reality or gaining special powers, not even about being "spiritual," although all of these things may happen as a by-product to meditation practice. It's about becoming acquainted with ourselves. Nevertheless, many other straightforward benefits do come from meditation. You can concentrate better and put your mind where you want it. You can see yourself as you become attached to a thought—whether that thought is fear, despair, anger, or delight. Very slowly, over the years, the places where you get stuck emotionally and mentally are worn away by your practice of awareness. You come to be more resilient. Ultimately, as you become more aware of your nature—of who you are—you become more compassionate.

The most powerful aspect of Zen practice is the freedom it gives you. Zen goes directly to your own experience of the oneness of the universe, of your interconnectedness with all things. You learn to distrust whatever you clung to in your old sense of separation, and that realization can be the most liberating thing in your life, a freedom beyond anything you could have imagined.

To achieve this kind of freedom, you need to give yourself the best possible chance of continuing in the practice. Begin by doing three things: Start meditating (instructions are given in chapter 2). Read a book (chapter 10 lists books that are especially valuable for people new to Zen). Find a sangha, a community to practice with (chapters 4 and 11 will help you find a group). If you do these three things, you will have taken the first steps to genuine practice. Sounds simple? It is simple, but it's not easy. The more your practice deepens, the more you will be challenged—and rewarded—by the elegance of the practice and by your own mind.

2

The Gateways to Realization

MEDITATION

AND KOANS

The bell sounds once. You sit in stillness as your attention contracts and converges within the bell's timbre. The bell sounds again. Your attention expands, carried by the bell's resonance outward in spaciousness. The bell sounds a third time. Your attention is drawn inward with your breath. One. Inhaling, you feel the cool air in your nostrils and filling you. Two. The breath is warm and coarse as you exhale. For a moment, you experience a sense of euphoria, but you are sitting too high on your zafu, and your raised knees cause pain in your hips. You make a small gassho bow and move forward on your cushion. The movement is no different from the countless adjustments you make throughout your daily life to avoid discomfort—physical or mental—except that this time you are aware of it. One.

ZAZEN

WHEN YOU SIT down to meditate, whether you are in the formal setting of a hushed zendo or on a cushion in your own home, you are within the heart of Zen Buddhism. Some practitioners may skip services or other parts of Zen practice, but Zen is not Zen without zazen, "the mind that sits." Dogen, the thirteenth-century Japanese master who founded the Soto school, called zazen the Dharma Gate of Joy and Comfort—the gateway to practice, to realization. Dogen stressed that when we practice wholeheartedly with our complete body and mind, practice and realization are the same thing. Dogen saw zazen not as a vehicle for attaining enlightenment but as enlightenment itself. We do not need to search for some exotic state that we'll eventually achieve. Rather, just that process—just sitting

down—is *it*, is the realization of this moment, of this life. Meditation is thus what holds our spiritual practice together.

It's easy to lose touch with how amazing the experience of simply sitting is—not in order to become enlightened but just in order to sit zazen. Human nature

A Buddha image placed on a windowsill is the home altar for this meditator.

being what it is, soon after we discover how blissful sitting meditation can be, we begin to separate from the experience of it and see it as something we *ought* to do. We call it a discipline, and it becomes fraught with difficulties. But Dogen also saw zazen as a "protection," something that takes care of us and nourishes us. And this foundation of our practice, nourishing and enlightening, is very simple to do.

POSTURE AND CLOTHING

Each time you sit down to meditate, you are reenacting the Buddha's enlightenment experience. The Buddha himself instructed his followers to go into a forest and to sit down under a tree, but few of us living in the complex modern world have the opportunity to do that literally. Ideally, you should find a quiet place in your home where you can sit each day. If you live in the middle of unavoidable noise, however, that's a fine situation for practice too. The important thing is to not resist the noise but to be where you are within the moment.

Clothing

It's helpful to be dressed comfortably when you meditate. If you can, wear loose clothes, especially garments that do not fit tightly around your knees. Binding clothes can cause strain and tension in your body. At most Zen centers, you'll see people wearing meditation robes, which lessen distraction and are considered tools for the work of meditation.

Sitting Position

You want to find a position that's stable and comfortable and at the same time allows you to be alert. Traditionally, people have sat cross-legged on the floor with two cushions. One large cushion, about one and a half by three feet, is essentially a mat, or *zabuton;* the second cushion, or *zafu,* is much smaller and is often round. (When you begin to practice, you can improvise by using a folded blanket and a bed pillow doubled over.) Sit on the forward third of your zafu, using it as a wedge that pushes your knees down onto the floor and gives you a balanced position. You form a tripod with your two knees and your buttocks. If you sit in the middle or top of the cushion, your knees will go up, you'll be unbalanced, and your legs may go to sleep. Rock back and forth and to the side several times to warm up your legs and get your balance. Then sit erectly—but not stiffly tense—so that your spine is straight and your ears align with your shoulders. Imagine that the top of your spine is attached to a string; tug gently on the string to straighten your spine.

You can choose one of three possible cross-legged positions: the full lotus *(kekkafuza),* the half lotus *(hankafuza),* and simply crossed legs, or the Burmese position. Because the full lotus posture is the most stable position, you should use it if you can: Sitting on your zafu, first put your right foot, sole up, on your left thigh. Then place your left foot, sole up, on your right thigh. As Zen master Shunryu Suzuki, who founded the Zen Center of San Francisco, has noted, in this position the right and left leg have become one, expressing the important Zen teaching of oneness, of nonduality.

If you are unable to assume the full lotus posture, try the half lotus: Place your right foot, sole up, on your left thigh, but fold your left leg in front of you so that your left foot is on the floor. If the half lotus too is impossible, try the Burmese position: Sit with your legs folded and crossed in front of you, so that the sides of both feet touch the floor or your zabuton. Do

The full lotus *(kekkafuza)*.
Rest your right foot on the left thigh, and your left foot on the right thigh.

not cross one leg on top of the other, which can cause one or both feet to go to sleep. You can alternate the outside leg if you wish. Although all of the cross-legged positions may be unpleasant in the beginning, the longer you practice meditation, the more flexible your legs will become and the less painful these positions will be.

If you simply are not very limber and find all cross-legged positions distractingly uncomfortable, you can try a kneeling position. In *seiza*, which is the traditional position for meditation in Japan, first kneel with your knees apart, then sit back on your heels, keeping your spine erect. If this position stresses your knees too much, you can try the alternative known as riding a horse. For this position, again kneel with your knees apart, put a cushion on edge between your legs and under your bottom, and sit back on it. As another alternative, some people are most comfortable using a three-piece meditation or seiza bench: a slanted plank about 8 inches wide and 12 inches long, supported

The half lotus *(hankafuza). Rest your right foot on the left thigh, while the left foot rests on the floor.*

The Burmese position. *Fold both legs in front of your body, but do not cross them over each other.*

by two side planks about 8 inches high. For this position, kneel with your knees close together, place the bench so that it straddles your legs, and sit back on it with your spine erect.

If none of these positions works for you, there's absolutely nothing wrong with sitting in a chair. If you do use a chair, sit on the forward third of the seat, and try not to lean back or slouch against the back of the chair. Keep your feet far enough apart that you feel balanced. If your feet do not easily reach the floor, by all means put a cushion under them so that you are stable.

Regardless of whether you are sitting on a cushion, a bench, or a chair, keep your spine straight, as if the back of your head were suspended from the ceiling by that imaginary string, with your ears and shoulders aligned. The basic goal of all of these positions is to find a way to sit that is so stable that you

Seiza. *Kneeling with knees apart, sit back on your heels.*

The horse. *Kneeling with knees apart, put your zafu on end under your buttocks and sit back on it.*

Using a seiza bench. *Keep your legs close together, so that the side panels of the bench straddle them, and sit back on the bench.*

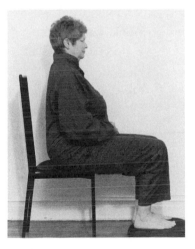

Using a chair. *Sit far enough forward that you are not tempted to slouch against the back of the chair.*

don't have to move for about thirty minutes. There's nothing intrinsically good about not moving—later we'll turn to kinhin, walking meditation—but when you move your body or mind, you may distract yourself from your practice. And if you collapse into a contorted posture, you may look quite profound—but as Kosho Uchiyama notes in *Opening the Hand of Thought,* that posture won't do much for your practice:

> Compare the zazen posture to Rodin's famous statue *The Thinker.* It sounds good to say "thinking," but actually *The Thinker* exemplifies a posture of chasing after illusions. The figure sits hunched over, his shoulders drawn forward and his chest compressed. The arms and legs are bent, the neck and fingers are bent, and even the toes are bent. When our body is bent like this, blood becomes congested and we get caught up in our imagination and become unable to break free. On the other hand, when we sit zazen, everything is straight—trunk, back, neck, and head. Because our abdomen rests comfortably on solidly folded legs, blood leaves the head and circulates plentifully toward the abdomen. Precisely because blood circulates downward from the head, congestion is alleviated, excitability is lessened, and we no longer need chase after fantasies and delusions. Therefore, doing correct zazen means taking the correct posture and entrusting everything to it.

Head

With your ears aligned with your shoulders, lower your chin slightly. This will straighten your spine and relax your jaw. Do not tuck your chin in so tightly that you create tension in your throat. This posture will also aid you in holding your eyes in the proper position.

Eyes

Keep your eyes open—in Zen, we're very focused on being where we are, not on being inside our heads. But because strong light as well as your surroundings can be distracting, look down toward the floor about two or three feet in front of your body. Just by looking down in that way, your eyelids close slightly. Let your focus soften, so that you are not really looking at anything.

Mouth

Place your tongue against the roof of your mouth, just where your teeth and your gums meet. This position helps prevent excessive salivation.

Hands

Place your hands in what's called the *cosmic mudra*: Your active hand (your right hand if you're right-handed), palm up, cradles your passive hand, and your thumbs meet about an inch below your navel, forming an oval in front of the part of your abdomen known as the *hara*, believed to be the spiritual center of human beings. Your arms or wrists may rest lightly on your thighs. This hand position itself becomes part of your awareness when you meditate. When you drift away on the wings of thought, your hands may collapse on your lap and your thumbs may nose-dive into your palms or begin a shoving match against each other— a sure sign that your body is tense. Mindfulness of your hand position, as of all of your body, is a

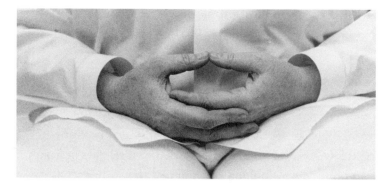

Cosmic mudra *(dhyani mudra). With your active hand—in this case, the right hand of a right-handed meditator—cradle the passive hand, while the thumbs form an oval about an inch below the waist, in front of the area known as the hara.*

very important part of meditation, as Shunryu Suzuki, in *Zen Mind, Beginner's Mind,* noted:

> The most important point is to own your own physical body. If you slump, you will lose your self. Your mind will be wandering about somewhere else; you will not be in your body. This is not the way. We must exist right here, right now! . . . When we have our body and mind in order, everything else will exist in the right place, in the right way.

When you have your body in order, you are ready to begin to practice the art of meditation.

BEGINNING ZAZEN

With your hands in the cosmic mudra, concentrate on the hara. Breathe in normally through your nose, imagining that you are filling with air a balloon that's located in the hara. When you breathe out, deflate that balloon. This is essentially the kind of breathing done in zazen: in through the nose gently, all the way down to the hara, then back up.

Don't try to force deep breaths or small breaths or to control your breathing in any way. In Zen the important thing is to be *aware* of each breath—to just watch it happening. When you let your breath move in and out, some breaths naturally will be very deep and some will be rather shallow. Sometimes you may even have difficulty finding your breath, and you may need to rely on the subtle movement of the hara to locate it.

After you've settled into a pattern of breathing, begin to count: *one* with the inbreath and *two* with the outbreath, then *three* with the next inbreath and *four* with the next outbreath. Continue counting until you get to *ten*. Then go back to *one* and continue this practice. Of if you prefer, count *one* with the outbreath, then *two* with the inbreath. Some people find that it's easier to focus on the breath if the initial movement is to breathe out, to empty out, on *one*. See which one works best for you.

Counting to *ten* sounds simple, but it's almost impossible to do, especially when you are just beginning to practice. What actually happens is that you continue counting until you have a thought—until you realize that you're not really counting anymore but rather are thinking about something. The instant you realize that you're thinking about something else, acknowledge that thought, let it go, and return to *one*. Your process might go something like: Breathing in, you count *one*. Exhaling, you count *two*. Inhaling, you think, "This isn't so hard. I'm pretty good at this. I bet I could be a meditation teacher sooner or later." Then you realize that you're not counting *three* but are thinking about something. At that point, you recognize that thought: "Oh, I was having a thought about how good I am." Let the thought go, and return to *one*. Again, you inhale and count *one*. You exhale and count *two*. You inhale, and as you inhale you think, "What am I going to do after this meditation period? I think I'd better call my friend to see if we can go out for a . . ." There's no telling how long it will be before you realize that you're not counting but planning. So you recognize the thought "I'm planning," then you let that thought go and return to *one* again.

A similar phenomenon of mindlessness is to continue counting—way past *ten*—while you are thinking. When you solve that work problem as you count *thirty-eight,* smile at the realization and start again at *one*.

That's the way our practice usually goes when we begin to meditate—and often for long after we begin. In the process, we start to see all the different ways the mind behaves. We learn that we have a so-called *monkey mind*—a mind that's running around and swinging from tree to tree. In even our first sitting, we begin to tether that monkey when we say, "Oh, this is what I'm doing," and go back to *one*.

When we take up meditation, most of us are quite surprised by how our minds leap from one thing to the next to the next. After six months or so of practice, we begin to realize that in fact our minds go to only seven or eight or ten grooves—our typical patterns of thought. At this point, we become less impressed with the breadth and diversity of our thoughts and more aware of how repetitive they are. It's as if the monkey goes to only a few particular trees. Although it's still a monkey mind, it's a mind that leaps only to the pear tree, to the apple tree, to the complaining tree, to the planning tree, and to the judgment tree. As disconcerting as monkey mind may be, it's not a "bad" monkey mind—it is the normal way the mind works, and *practice is to be aware of the way the mind works*. In the beginning, if this gamboling mind baffles and frustrates you, try imagining that your mind is a toddler who starts to wander out into the street. You don't hit the toddler. You don't grab her so hard that you dislocate her arm. You just gently round her up and point her in another direction. That's the way you need to treat yourself.

It's very important to simply practice without judging your practice. You'll experience a great hindrance if you think you *should* get to *ten* and will feel you've failed when you don't. The examples given above are very common. The point is not to get to *ten*—counting to ten is arbitrary, simpler than counting to one hundred. The point is to know what you're doing with your mind. The moment you realize that you're not counting is the moment that you come back to the now. "I'm here" is an instant of enlightenment, of complete awareness. Be joyful that you've discovered it, rather than saying, "Oh, no. I've failed again."

If you were to sit absolutely still and not have any thoughts, you would be much like the rock described by Zen master Uchiyama in *Opening the Hand of Thought*:

Imagine placing a large rock next to a person doing zazen. Since this rock is not alive, no matter how long it sits there, a thought will never occur to it. Unlike the rock, however, the person doing zazen is a living human being. Even if we sit as stationary as the rock, we cannot say that no thoughts will occur. On the contrary, if they did not, we would have to say that that person is no longer alive. But, of course, the truth of life never means to become lifeless like the rock. For that reason, thoughts ceasing to occur is not the ideal state of one sitting zazen.

THE · DROPPING · AWAY · OF · BODY · AND · MIND

With continued practice, eventually you become quieter, the mind becomes less and less disturbed, and you begin to get in touch with a deep level of your awareness and your consciousness. This very powerful aspect of meditation is an appreciation of your oneness with all things—sometimes expressed by Dogen and others as "the dropping away of body and mind." Your body becomes so still that you are no longer concerned with it. Your mind becomes so still that you draw close to an awareness of who you really are. Shunryu Suzuki, in *Zen Mind, Beginner's Mind,* described what happens this way:

> When we practice zazen our mind always follows our breathing. When we inhale, the air comes into the inner world. When we exhale, the air goes out to the outer world. The inner world is limitless, and the outer world is also limitless. We say "inner world" or "outer world," but actually there is just one whole world. In this limitless world, our throat is like a swinging door. The air comes in and goes out like someone passing through a swinging door. If you think, "I breathe," the "I" is extra. There is no you to say "I." What we call "I" is just a swinging door which moves when we inhale and when we exhale. It just moves; that is all. When your mind is pure and calm enough to follow this movement, there is nothing: no "I," no world, no mind nor body; just a swinging door.

When we approach a falling away of body and mind, we may become a little frightened by it. And when we become frightened by it, we often move our body. The effort to not move during meditation is not some form of masochistic torture but rather an attempt to create the physical stillness that will permit us to experience a deepening practice. It also is a recognition that if we move every time we feel discomfort when we sit, we probably also spend much of our lives literally or figuratively moving to get away from aversive situations. Yet the effort to not move itself often causes us further discomfort.

Physical Discomfort

Sitting in excruciating pain has the same effect on meditation as moving does. It's a distraction. When you first become aware of discomfort, try to not move right away. Understand that you *can* change your position, but take a few moments to see how you react to the discomfort. Very often the discomfort will go away when you do that, especially the annoyance of a nose or ear that's itching. Just leave it alone. That itch will go away, and the other ear or something else will start to itch. What you're experiencing is just the body letting go of tension. If you can stay with the pain or itch, eventually it will change—for better or worse—because nothing stays the same for very long.

Sometimes when you bring a pain into awareness, it simply disappears. But sometimes it gets worse, probably because you are unconsciously tensing up around it. If you find that the discomfort is too great—shooting pains in a knee that don't go away after three or four minutes, for example—then *prepare* to move. Whether you're sitting in a group or alone, make a little bow, a *gassho* bow, to punctuate your practice and ensure that you don't get sloppy and constantly move. Make the bow, then make the necessary adjustment to your body, then begin sitting again.

Through practice you will stretch your muscles so that physical pain requiring movement occurs less and less frequently. Even after you've been practicing for some time, however, you may find that your feet or legs continue to go to sleep. But unless you have a medical problem, just let it happen for as long as you're sitting, then be very careful not to stand up until you have feeling in your feet or legs again.

Emotional Unease

The discomfort experienced during sitting may not just be physical. Many of us have spent years building up emotional armor, and we find it difficult to allow ourselves to become completely vulnerable during this dropping-away process. Even though we may consciously want to allow the body and mind to fall away, some part of us may still be holding on, and resistance develops. It may be physiological—your nose itches, you scratch it, and suddenly you're in a completely different place than you were a split second ago. Or perhaps you're in the midst of deep silence when a distracting thought comes up, you connect with the thought, and you're gone—enmeshed in ordinary thinking. Tears may well up—or laughter. Both are normal and can be acknowledged and released.

For most of us, beginning to sit is empowering: We see what our thoughts are like, and it's exciting to be able to relinquish them. But as we begin to go deeper, our practice may become a little scary at times. Again, be easy with yourself. Nothing that you learn about how your mind works is going to hurt you.

Contemporary Zen master Dainin Katagiri, in *Returning to Silence*, compares the state of your meditative mind to the dynamic but still center of a ball:

> A ball is constantly changing, rolling, acting. This is human life. Human beings never stop acting. Whatever you are doing—sitting, sleeping, even standing still—you are still acting. Without action, you do not exist. It is just like a ball that is constantly going here and there or standing still according to circumstances. When a slope comes, the ball rolls down the hill. It acts, but even though it appears to be moving, the center is always still. We call this stillness *samadhi* [single-pointed focus, as on the breath].

A DAILY PRACTICE

We may be powerfully drawn to the idea of meditation, but when it comes to actually sitting, we are frequently teeming with excuses about how we feel or how many other demands there are on our time. Often our thoughts go something like this: "I'm just so tired that I'd probably fall asleep anyway. Why bother? I'd be better off just going to bed and getting some rest." Or "I know I would feel better if I sat this morning, but I'd be worrying the whole time about getting to work on time. I just don't have time to do it right." How long does it take "to do it right"? And how often?

Buddhism arose in Asia, where monastics generally meditate according to set patterns. At sesshins and other types of Zen retreats, meditation schedules are usually prescribed. But in the West, where so many practitioners are laypeople, there is no set schedule for when to meditate and for how long. An experienced meditator might meditate once or twice a day for 45 to 60 minutes, but here are a few guidelines for a beginner:

1. If you can, meditate 15 minutes a day in the beginning.
2. If you can't do that, meditate once a day for as long as you can.
3. If you can't do that, leave your cushion between your bed and the bathroom, and promise yourself that once a day (perhaps when you get up or go to bed) you will sit down on your cushion and assume a meditative posture whether you meditate or not.

You'll notice that in each of these suggestions, the most important thing for a beginner is to sit every day—preferably at the same time, for a set period, no matter how short. As we'll discuss in chapter 3, a daily practice is greatly supported by joining a local sitting group and attending sesshins.

THE COUNTING of the breath is a traditional introductory practice, often done by students as their only practice for a year or so after they take up meditation, but it is not just a beginner's practice. Many experienced

Meditators doing zazen.

meditators do this calming, steadying practice when they first sit down, before they undertake another practice. After beginning students have spent some months counting their breath, they often take up a practice called following the breath, where the counting is stopped, but the attention is still with the breath as it goes down and comes back. Students drop away the counting to see if attention can be maintained. If concentration is still good, the teacher and student, usually in a private interview called *dokusan*, discussed in chapter 4, together determine what might be the best next practice. Generally, it will be either koan study or *shikantaza*.

KOAN STUDY

After you have developed a stable meditation practice, can maintain concentration, and have a degree of awareness and mindfulness, your teacher may introduce you to a *koan*, a paradoxical phrase or story that transcends logic. Buddhist scholar Christmas Humphreys compared a koan to a pebble in the mouth of a man wandering in the desert: "It does not quench existing thirst, but it stimulates the means of quenching it."

Koans are most frequently used in the Rinzai Zen tradition, but Soto Zen teachers may also use them. Because koans can be very destabilizing—that's one of their functions—you must have developed a certain amount of stability before beginning this practice, and koan study should be undertaken only with a teacher.

Koans emerged as a formal system of teaching during the mid-tenth century in China out of ordinary interactions between teachers and students while they were on pilgrimages or working or living together in monasteries. Then the stories would be told to another generation: "This is what happened to Joshu. Someone asked Joshu if he thought a dog had Buddha-nature and he said, 'Mu.' What do you think of that?" In this way, an everyday occurrence became a teaching story, a koan (literally "public notice," in Japanese).

In koan study, your teacher gives you a koan such as "What is the sound of one hand clapping?" or "What was your face before your mother and father were born? Don't tell me—show me." Often the first koan that teachers give students is that famous and enigmatic koan of Joshu's answer, *Mu.* (*Mu* can mean many different things, including "no.") Another popular koan for early study is "If you meet the Buddha on the road, kill the Buddha." This koan forces beginning students to confront their own tradition's and culture's ideas about what Zen Buddhist practice is: Anytime they see something they think is the Buddha and it is external to them, they must get rid of it. The koan doesn't mean to kill the teacher or senior students in the sangha or images on the altar. Rather, the function of this koan is to help students to kill their preconceived ideas so that they can experience the truth freshly.

When a teacher has given you a koan, it is up to you to work with the paradoxical expression and to come up with a satisfactory presentation of its meaning for your teacher. The challenge is to learn to work with your whole body and mind, not just your intellect. Most of us don't know how to work with our full consciousness of this moment, so we have to learn to do it.

When you take up koan study, begin your zazen period with a few minutes of counting breaths until you are stable and can imagine yourself as a container of silence. Then simply drop the koan into that container, and do *not* seek an answer. Just be intimate with the koan. Become the koan. Don't seek an answer until you're in the room with your teacher, then see what comes up. Is this an impossible instruction? Perhaps, but it will bring you much closer to the intimacy required by a koan than will reading or analyzing or considering this answer or that. A practiced answer may sound all right, but it doesn't make you one with the koan—and your teacher will see through your attempt to look good.

Teachers generally adhere to an injunction against explaining too much about koans, and there are many koans that demonstrate how dangerous it is to have someone explain a koan to you. Such explanations take away from you the opportunity to have the insight. If you become satisfied with the words—even the few words just said about "When you see the Buddha"—then you've been robbed of the experience of understanding it for yourself. Zen Buddhist teachers are thus very reluctant to talk about koans, because doing so essentially destroys one of the most powerful tools they use with their students. In *Awakening to Zen*, Roshi Philip Kapleau tells a story that well illustrates the futility of explanation for certain types of experiences:

> Concert pianist Vladimir Horowitz tells about the time he played a dissonant contemporary composition at a private gathering. When he had finished, someone asked, "I just don't understand what that composition means, Mr. Horowitz. Could you please explain?" Without a word, Horowitz played the composition again, turned to his questioner, and announced, "That's what it means!"

Koan study must be done with a Zen Buddhist teacher or spiritual guide. If you try to work with koans alone or with someone who hasn't studied koans and has not experienced them, the study goes nowhere and has no power at all. In a common Buddhist description, most of us are like a person carrying a board on one shoulder: We can see only to one side, so our tendency is either to always see the oneness of everything or to always see the difference of everything. The key to insightful practice is to be able to have our consciousness move back and forth flawlessly between understanding and experiencing both the unity and the diversity of the universe.

Sometimes a teacher might accept a particular response on a koan from one student but reject the same response from another student. There is a definite relational aspect to koan study. The teacher's role is to allow the koans "to open" the student, and each student has a different "mind lock" to be opened. Many koans are about exploding our ideas of what Buddhism is, of what practice is, of what enlightenment is—they induce us to see that Buddhism, practice, and enlightenment are all right here, present, in our lives already. Other koans are aimed at creating more intimacy with things around us, called the *Dharmakaya,* or the unity of the Buddha's existence with all things. Can you become a tree threatened by acid rain? Can you become a farm worker who is not being paid and is losing immigration status? Many koans are about learning to experience these kinds of different aspects of reality.

Koan study is a very powerful practice in terms of pushing people into a deeper understanding of who they are. There's nothing quite like the experience of going to your teacher, making a presentation, being told no, and having the koan explode in your mind when you're on the way out the door. Or you might be washing dishes the next day, not even thinking of the koan, when suddenly you get it. It's like a door that opens into ourselves.

SHIKANTAZA

After you have developed a strong meditation practice through counting the breath, the teacher and you might decide that the best next step for you is to go deeper into silent sitting, or *shikantaza* (literally "nothing but precise sitting" in Japanese). Shikantaza is the purest form of zazen, and when you practice it, you use none of the supports—such as counting your breath or working with koans—that you may have used early in your practice.

To begin shikantaza, when you first sit down, stabilize your practice with a few minutes of counting the breath and try to relax deeply. Then begin shikantaza: just sitting. You can't do it wrong. Allow whatever comes up to come up, whether it's a sound or a thought or a physical sensation. Observe it, and let it drop away. Don't get caught up in your thoughts, but just allow whatever is present to be present. From the moment you begin to do shikantaza, you are performing a practice of enlightenment. Shikantaza can be your practice for as long as you live—most Zen teachers do shikantaza—but there's not much to say about it. Over time you will become increasingly aware of its subtleties, and if you have a meeting with your teacher while you're practicing shikantaza, just talk about whatever important issues are arising in your practice.

MEDITATION TECHNIQUES—zazen, koans, shikantaza—are not regimens that have to be enforced in a brutal fashion. Rather, they are skillful means to attain the joy and insight of wisdom. They do require a certain amount of discipline of the body and mind, but it should be a soft and resilient discipline that allows your body and mind to be different today from the way they were yesterday or even a moment ago. Continuing practice will help you to develop a kinetic strength that allows you to sit in absolute stillness. Then your body and mind fall away, and what is left is everything that you are.

3

A World of Stillness and Order

THE

ZENDO

Stepping into the zendo, you enter a world of tranquillity. There's nothing here to greatly divert you—you're away from the distracting differences of everything else in the world. In the soft light filtering through ricepaper screens, you see identical cushions carefully aligned along the side walls and an altar at the far end. As your eyes adjust to the light, you distinguish on the altar a Buddha image, a flower, and several small bowls. You bow and prepare to sit zazen. You are immersed in peace.

YOU MAY BEGIN your meditation practice in a quiet area in your own home, but sooner or later you will probably want to look for a Zen center near you, so that your practice will have the support of a *sangha* (a Buddhist community) and the direction of a teacher. How often should you sit at home, and how often should you try to sit at a zendo? It's difficult to

describe what an ideal practice might be for you. What's ideal—or even possible—really depends upon the circumstances of each individual's life. If you are a young student with few commitments, you can shape a practice that is very different from what you can manage if you have a demanding work or family situation. And if you live far from a Zen center, you may need to start your own sitting group, an undertaking described in chapter 4.

Generally, you should try to sit at home each morning and/or evening. If possible, also try to sit with a sangha for an hour once a week and for a full day each month. If your circumstances permit, you may also take a week-long sesshin, or retreat, one or more times a year. The opportunities for these different practices vary considerably from person to person and from geographical area to area. Some people sit with their sangha three times a week, while others only sit alone. Some take four sesshins a year, while others do not go on retreats at all. Over time your practice will take shape according to the other demands in your life and your own desires. In the beginning, it's most important to put your efforts into developing your own meditation practice and to finding a zendo where you can practice with others.

WHAT KIND OF ZENDO?

As interest in Zen Buddhism has increased, the number of laypeople seeking places to practice and attend sesshins has led to the rapid growth of Zen centers all around the country. (For a list of some of the zendos in the United States and abroad, see chapter 11.) Some are large, some are small; some are rural, some are urban. Each has its own distinct personality, and the few centers described here can give you an idea of the diversity of kinds of centers that you might find near your home.

On the Maine coast, not far from Acadia National Park, the Morgan Bay Zendo nestles on an often fog-bound hillside. Built several decades ago in the Japanese style, with many materials brought from Japan, the small center has a zendo with its own reflecting pool, a dining and meeting hall with kitchen and shower facilities, several small cabins, and a tranquil moss garden deep in the woods, ideal for kinhin. Although there is not currently a resident teacher—the zendo is maintained by a lay board of directors—it has zazen sittings twice weekly from May to December, work days, and retreats of from one to five days with visiting teachers. In the summer, retreatants often tent-camp in sites mowed into a field of wildflowers.

Near Woodstock, New York, in the far different but equally beautiful rural setting of the Catskill Mountains, is the imposing Zen Mountain Monastery (ZMM), founded by Roshi John Daido Loori. Its 235 acres have been declared a nature sanctuary, and the turn-of-the-century white oak and bluestone main building has been designated a national historic landmark. ZMM offers a variety of training programs, lasting from one day to one year. The monthly residential-weekend "Introduction to Zen Training" is especially valuable for those new to

Morgan Bay Zendo. *This center (top), near Surry, Maine, has a zendo for meditation (on left) as well as a hall that can be used for meals (on right). The zendo was built using traditional materials from Japan. Inside (above), the altar (right) has the traditional candle, water, incense, flower, and statue of Manjushri (Wisdom)—but also a statue of Kannon, or Kuan-yin, the female manifestation of Compassion.*

Zen Mountain Monastery.
This large center in Mount Tremper, New York, accommodates monastics and lay residents for retreats and workshops lasting from one day to one year. Abbot John Daido Loori is a successor to Hakuyu Taizan Maezumi Roshi, whose photograph is on the altar.

Zen. There are also monthly sesshins, as well as a variety of training programs, including residential training for those in the arts and those with interests in writing, painting, archery, environmental issues, and even birding.

A dramatically contrasting zendo is Zen Mountain Monastery's affiliate the Zen Center of New York City (ZCNYC), under the supervision of Bonnie Myotai Treace, sensei and vice-abbess of Zen Mountain Monastery. Despite its location on the tenth (top) floor of a commercial office building in midtown Manhattan, when you step through the doorway into the zendo, you're enveloped in the same soothing stillness you would find at a zendo in the most isolated forest. The ZCNYC offers zazen on weeknights, on two weekday mornings, and on Sunday, along with a service and Dharma talk. On Sundays, too, there is a training program for those new to Zen. Other programs at ZCNYC include Eight Gates training for advanced students and Saturday workshops on such subjects as ikebana, urban haiku, and Right Livelihood businesses. ZCNYC's relationship with Zen Mountain Monastery links it to residential training programs there.

Perhaps the most symbolic of the American zendos mentioned here is Stone Creek Zendo, in Sebastopol, California. Built, literally, by resident teacher Rev. Jisho Warner in a traditional Japanese style with American materials, it opened in December 1996 and was dedicated in June 1997 at an outdoor ceremony led by Rev. Tozen Akiyama of the Milwaukee Zen Center and including Rev. Karen Sunna of the Minnesota Zen Meditation Center. Stone Creek Zendo has morning and evening zazen sessions four times a week, monthly all-day sittings or sesshins, and study groups and training in making *rakusus,* the rectangular patchwork symbolizing the Buddha's

Zen Center of New York City.
Students come for periods of meditation in a zendo that overlooks urban high-rises. On Sundays, Bonnie Myotai Treace, Sensei, holds introductory sessions, services, and zazen.

Stone Creek Zendo.
Built by its resident teacher in Sebastopol, California, this is one of the newer Zen centers in the United States. At its dedication (above), resident teacher Rev. Jisho Warner (right) gasshos and welcomes Rev. Tozen Akiyama (left) of the Milwaukee Zen Center and Rev. Karen Sunna (center) of the Minnesota Zen Meditation Center.

robes, worn by initiates (lay and monastic) who have taken formal Buddhist vows. It is very moving to enter this small light-bathed zendo, to see the lined-up zafus, the Buddha statue, the flowers—and to be quietly enfolded in both its newness and its timelessness. You will find this peace in any zendo you enter, no matter where it is.

VISITING A ZENDO

Your first visit to a *zendo*, a hall where zazen is formally practiced, may fill you with anticipation—and a bit of anxiety about how to behave in this unfamiliar environment. Telephone ahead to find out the best time for your first visit; many zendos have set times for introductory sessions for beginners, which will make your entry quite easy. Once you get to a zendo, it's simple: Just observe other people mindfully, and do what they do. The heart of Zen teaching is to learn through the body in awareness, so if you're unsure about what to do, you are fully within Zen tradition to learn by just following what others around you are doing. Unless the zendo is in an urban high-rise—in which case, the entrance may be a little different—here's what you'll probably find:

In a large monastery or large Zen center, there are different rooms or buildings for different purposes. Meditation is done in the Zen room, or zendo; services, in the Buddha hall; and Dharma (teaching) talks, in the Dharma hall. In smaller Zen communities, one hall, usually referred to as the zendo, serves all these ends.

Before you enter the zendo, take off your shoes and place them on the shoe rack or shelves outside, because inside you'll

Just outside of zendos, shelves are provided for shoes and personal belongings.

be putting your feet on cushions where people sit. Leave your coat and other belongings in the place provided—usually in a Dharma community there's so much trust that women don't carry even their purses to their cushions.

Outside the door, you'll find a bell used to call people to services and for other ritual functions. You'll also usually find a *han,* a wooden board that is struck to call people to sitting periods throughout the day in Zen monasteries. The han is an important accoutrement of a Zen center, for it gives a sharp, clear sound that can be heard up to a half mile away. Traditionally, different patterns of striking the han are used to let people know how long it is until the sitting begins. If you go to a Zen center in the country, you might hear a *bok,* then perhaps thirty seconds later another *bok,* and you know that you've got about five minutes to get to the zendo. As the time for sitting gets nearer, the *boks* get closer and closer together. In an urban setting, the same pattern exists, but the spaced *boks* can become a virtual drumroll in less than a minute.

All you have to do is enter and take your seat.

TAKING YOUR SEAT

When you go into a Japanese Zen temple or a very traditional American zendo, enter with your left foot first, and do a standing bow with your hands at your waist. From the cushions neatly lined up along the wall, select one that is not occupied, and slowly walk clockwise around the room to it. With your palms together in front of you in gassho (see photograph, page 53), bow in sequence to the image on the altar, to your cushion, and to the person at the opposite side of the room. In many zendos,

The han, hanging just outside the zendo, is struck with a wooden mallet to call people to zazen periods.

if there are meditators at the cushions next to yours, they will bow to you when you bow. Then slowly take your seat facing either the wall or the center of the room if a period of zazen is about to begin, or continue standing if some kind of service is scheduled—again, do whatever other people are doing.

The tradition of the zendo and the time of day determine whether you sit facing the center of the room or facing the wall. In most American Soto Zen centers, you face the wall except when you are chanting or in sesshin. In Rinzai zendos, you face away from the wall.

THE ALTAR

In a zendo, the figure on the altar is often the embodiment of Wisdom, Manjushri, in whose hand a sword is poised to slash through delusions. (If there is a separate Buddha hall, the image there is likely to be the historical Buddha; if one hall is used for several purposes, the image may be either Manjushri or the Buddha.) Arrayed near this statue are vessels holding symbolic representations of the four elements: A small container holds *water,* the unwavering flame of a candle is *fire,* incense makes the *air* visible, and *earth* is manifest in a single flower or a modest arrangement.

There are usually several other objects on or near the altar. Symbolic of the sword of Manjushri is the *kyosaku* ("wake-up," or "encouragement," stick), a flattened stick about the size of a yardstick that is used to strike the shoulders, encouraging and stimulating people who have become tired or sleepy during long meditation periods. Despite widespread misconceptions, the kyosaku is never used for punishment, only for encouragement—it is even sometimes referred to as the compassion stick.

Meditators remain standing while they chant from the zendo's ritual book.

During sittings one of the senior students has the responsibility to walk around the zendo with the kyosaku. If a meditator has developed pain or tension across the shoulders and back and would like to be struck, he or she gasshos, and the person with the kyosaku bows back. The person who wishes to be struck offers one shoulder, then the other, and the person with the kyosaku respectfully strikes each shoulder on an acupressure point at the base of the neck. Then the two people bow to each other, and the person continues sitting. Although some Zen centers have discontinued kyosaku, many continue to use it.

Also on the altar is a box—a *hako*—for incense that's burned during services. Nearby in a small center that uses one room for all functions, there are books of *sutras* (Buddhist discourses) and chants that are used during services. Also near the altar are several bells and clappers, which are employed at various times as basic communications systems that indicate such things as when it's time to speed up or end a chant or when it's time for

The sword with which Manjushri slashes through delusions is echoed in the kyosaku, a meditation aid used to encourage those who may have become sleepy during long periods of zazen. Right: A meditator on the left raises his hands in gassho to invite the senior student with the kyosaku to approach.

the officiant to move in a particular way. Part of the training in a Zen group is to learn to use all the different instruments at the right time.

In almost all Buddhist traditions that perform services, there is *circumambulation,* where participants walk around the Buddha image on the altar or walk in a circle, representing reverence for the unity of all things. In centers where all services take place in the zendo, there is generally a decorated mat in front of the altar, in the center of the room. Whoever is officiating in the service may walk around that mat.

SITTING MEDITATION

At the beginning of a sitting period, the bell is rung three times. Usually there has been a lot of activity—people arriving, a business meeting, or a service, perhaps—and the energy seems to build until everyone takes a seat. Then a quiet descends, and an empty space waits for the three bells.

After the first bell ringing, settle onto your cushion and practice zazen just as you do in your own home. Continue sitting in stillness, trying not to move, until you hear the second of the two bells sounded at the end of a sitting, then gassho. When the sitting ends, don't jump right up, but take a moment to sway back and forth and get your bearings again. Because the Zen tradition exemplifies respect for the authority of the teacher, do not rise until the teacher has stood up—an act of respect for the teachings rather than old-style authoritarianism. Then rise slowly and follow what everyone else is doing. At this time, there may be a period of walking meditation.

WALKING MEDITATION

In Zen the structured walking meditation practice is called *kinhin*, which just means "walking." At zendos kinhin is done by the whole group, in a line or circle, following a period of sitting. It's not a break from meditation but rather is a different kind of meditation— one that complements zazen in stretching the muscles and enhancing circulation after sitting for a long period.

Kinhin. *Periods of walking meditation provide the opportunity for stretching tired muscles and also practicing mindfulness in a kind of activity that is part of our daily life.*

The first time you do kinhin at a zendo, observe closely what others are doing, because practices differ slightly from one temple to another. In general, after a bell is rung twice, you'll rise, fold your hands (as described below), and walk in a line very slowly for a few minutes, then faster.

Standing, your body should maintain the same alert posture that you held while sitting. Your spine should be erect, your ears aligned with your shoulders. Kinhin is done with eyes lowered so that you can maintain strong concentration. The same dignity that marked your sitting posture should be preserved when you begin walking.

Hands are usually folded in one of two ways, called *isshu* and *shashu*. You'll need to look at those around you to determine which hand is on the outside, because this detail also differs from one tradition to another. For both positions, make a fist of one hand, enclosing your thumb, and cover the top of the fist with your other palm and thumb. Hold your elbows at right angles and away from your body. In isshu both hands are turned downward, with your thumbs next to your chest, as shown on page 50; in shashu your hands are against your chest, with thumbs upward.

Some zendos begin kinhin with the left foot, others with the right. Begin by taking just a small step—about half the length of your foot—with each full cycle of the breath. You'll find that awareness drops away from wherever it was focused before—counting or koan or shikantaza—and now includes both the pressure of the foot on the floor and the cycle of inbreath and outbreath. After three or four minutes, you'll hear clackers (the sound of wood on wood), and you begin to walk in a normal or—depending upon the zendo and the group— quite a brisk pace. If you are practicing at a Rinzai zendo, you may be almost in a trot, but in the Soto tradition, the pace is more stately.

In both traditions, people walk following one another— together, as a community, rather than separately. Be mindful of the space created between you and the person in front of and behind you so that you're not walking on someone else's heels or holding the group up. You'll walk clockwise in a circle if you are inside the zendo or in a long line if you're outside. You'll usually walk for another seven or eight minutes —long enough to get the blood moving and to allow anyone who needs to to bow out of line, go to the bathroom, then return to their original place in the line. If you've been doing kinhin outside, when you return to the zendo, the line will probably walk clockwise once around the room before you return to your place, bow, and resume sitting.

Above: **Isshu.** *Make a fist of one hand, enclosing your thumb, and cover that fist with your other hand. Turn both hands downward with your thumbs next to your chest.*

Below: **Shashu.** *Make a fist of one hand, enclosing your thumb, and cover that fist with your other hand. Hold both hands against your chest, with thumbs turned upward.*

Kinhin teaches you how to move with a meditative mind and is a potentially powerful technique for actualizing your meditation in your day-to-day activities.

SERVICES AND RITUALS

Most American Zen communities continue the Japanese tradition of having some kind of scheduled services—chanting, bowing, invocations, offering of incense—in the morning, in the evening, and perhaps at midday. These services are an excellent way to enhance your sense of reverence and gratitude to the people who have maintained the teachings' continuity for more than 2,500 years, thus giving you the opportunity to learn and practice these teachings. The services also enable you to express feelings that come up when you're practicing deep meditation, see that you're part of all things, and develop great respect for all beings.

Americans are often extremely resistant to the services at first. Many come to Zen thinking it's some kind of psychological practice they're going to do with their mind, facing a wall. They're appalled when they discover robes and incense and bowing. If you respond this way too and can't immediately embrace the spiritual and reverential aspects, just look at the services as a good means to practice awareness, openness, and what Shunryu Suzuki called *beginner's mind*: the ability to meet every experience with the innocence of first inquiry.

There's mindfulness in even the smallest details—a particular way to hold a sutra book and bowing at appropriate times, for example. In a way, a service is a mindfulness practice that is not removed from meditation at all. In a chanting service, for

During services you have the opportunity to bring mindfulness to formal aspects of bowing and using ritual accoutrements in very precise ways.

instance, you are breathing, giving voice, resonating, and harmonizing with other members who are chanting in mindful awareness—it is a form of meditation that takes into account the resonance of the voice and rhythm. Chanting has a powerful ritual function, which is so important for human expression. Some of the main chants and texts used for services are given in chapter 7.

BOWING

Many Westerners find that bowing *(gassho)* and deep bowing, or prostrations, go most strongly against their cultural conditioning—usually because they do not understand these practices and mistake humility for humiliation. Just as the dignity of our sitting and walking postures is an expression of our respect for our own Buddha-nature, so too are the various forms of bowing.

Gassho is a slight bow used to express respect or gratitude or to greet another person. When you gassho to your cushion before zazen, you are expressing respect for the space that you will enter. To gassho, bring your palms together in front of your chest—signifying uniting all phenomenal elements—and incline your head forward slightly for a moment or two, with your eyes down. Gasshos punctuate many elements in a zendo—entering, taking your place, recognizing other meditators, ending zazen.

Prostrations are used much less frequently in the West than they are in Asia. But their purpose, like the gassho, is to express humility, reverence, and gratitude to a "Buddha figure"—whether that figure is a statue or a teacher—while eliciting at the same time an experience of our own Buddha-nature. If you

Gassho. *At the end of a chant, the practitioners prepare to gassho.*

Prostrations. *During Dharma combat (see page 71), two senior students perform prostrations before their teacher.*

are in a situation in which you will do prostrations—perhaps as part of services, at the beginning of an interview with a teacher in a very formal zendo, or as part of a "public" interview known as *Dharma combat* (see photograph, page 71)—here's what's expected: From a standing position, with dignity assume a kneeling position like that described in chapter 2 for the traditional Japanese meditation posture (seiza), and gassho. Leaning forward, extend your hands—palms upward—toward the figure; simultaneously touch your forehead to the floor, and raise your palms a few inches above your head, symbolically receiving the Buddha's feet in reverence and gratitude. Return to the seiza position and gassho, then return to a standing position. Prostrations are often performed in sets of three.

As practice deepens, many Zen students find that bowing becomes a moving expression of the internal transformations they are experiencing, and nurturing humility seems to be an especially valuable practice for Americans.

SESSHIN

....

While the Buddha was still alive, monks and nuns began the custom of gathering together each year for intensive study and practice with the Buddha or a senior disciple during the three-month rainy season, or monsoon. The earliest forest monasteries came into being for this purpose. Several hundred years later, the monastics had discovered that large caves found throughout sections of northern India were warmer and drier, and they met there, leaving behind, in some places, exceptional works of art on the walls. Over the centuries, as Buddhism spread from one country to another, the form of these "retreats" evolved within each culture. But always practitioners have recognized the need to periodically come together in a place where there are minimal distractions so that they can renew their practice.

Sesshins afford the remarkable opportunity for sustained periods of mindfulness, during sitting, walking, meals, and work periods.

In Japanese monasteries, *sesshins* are regularly scheduled periods of intensive practice, ranging from ten days to three months. In American Zen, however, in order to accommodate the many lay practitioners, sesshins often last for a six-day week, starting on Monday and ending on Sunday. Weekend sesshins usually start on Friday evening and end about midday on Sunday. Sesshins are an opportunity to deepen your practice and immerse yourself in meditation and mindful awareness. Whenever possible, they are residential, so you have the opportunity to see what monastic practice or retreat practice is like. And there's something quite wonderful about being able to get up in the middle of the night, brush your teeth, and go into the zendo to sit.

During a sesshin, remarkable energy is generated within the context of stillness, which is created by what you do and what you don't do: You maintain silence the whole time, and you keep your eyes down to avoid communicating and being distracted by looking at others. You and everyone else wear dark clothes, so that your attention is not diverted by reading each other's T-shirts. Everything is muted, and the lack of stimulus helps you to sustain concentration, whether you're in a meditation period, taking a break, eating a meal, or going to sleep. The silence in and of itself has a wonderful effect on the mind and deepens concentration.

Residential retreats usually begin on, say, a Friday evening about five P.M. with registration, settling in, and a light supper. At most zendos, on the first evening of a sesshin, before the formal sittings begin, there is an orientation session, so that all—newcomers and returnees—will know where to go, what to expect, and how to conduct themselves.

Most full days begin before dawn and follow this general schedule:

- o Morning: periods of zazen/kinhin, a service, a formal breakfast, a work period
- o Midmorning: periods of zazen/kinhin, a service, a formal lunch, a short rest period
- o Afternoon: periods of zazen/kinhin, a Dharma talk, a service, a very light snack, and a short period for rest or personal needs
- o Evening: periods of zazen/kinhin, bedtime

ZAZEN AND KINHIN

Meditation is usually done in blocks of three 35- to 45-minute sittings, broken by 10- to 15-minute periods of walking. Generally, three bells signal the beginning of a zazen period; two bells at the end mean that a period of kinhin is starting.

When you sit, you do zazen just as you do at home or in your sitting group. When you go to your first sesshin, however, you'll find that the opportunity for spending continuous days and nights in zazen—as well as the support of others who surround you and who practice, as you do, in silence—deepens and intensifies your experience beyond what you had known was possible.

Usually, the teacher sits with you for one zazen period, then is available for private interviews during the other meditation periods. These *dokusans,* which we'll discuss in more detail in chapter 4, are opportunities to bring up problems of practice or to make presentations if you are working on a koan.

Ceremonially taken meals, called *oryoki,* are served in silence in the zendo or in a dining room. The word *oryoki* originally referred to the combination begging/food bowl given to a monk or nun at ordination. Later it came to be used for the three to five nested bowls used at mealtime and, finally, for the meal itself. During sesshin meals, you will sit cross-legged on your cushion, with your eating bowls before you, and formally continue the emphasis on mindfulness, reverence, and gratitude as you chant, are served, and eat.

At your first meal, you'll become familiar with the details of oryoki at this sesshin. A typical first meal might follow this sequence: When everyone has entered the zendo and is seated on their cushions, the group chants the Three Treasures (see page 112), then quietly unwraps the nested bowls and chopsticks provided to them for the sesshin. Another short chant usually follows before the food is ladled into your bowls. When you have been served but before you begin to eat, there will be a brief chant of gratitude for all who have raised, prepared, and served the meal, making it possible. Finally, in some zendos you will take six to eight grains from your rice bowl and put them into a special vessel as an offering for those in all realms who are hungry.

The nourishing meals will be vegetarian, usually consisting of rice, vegetables, and pickles, and are themselves an opportunity for meditation. Eat slowly and quietly, staying with your breath or with the taste and texture of the food. Those who served you will return to the hall; if you wish another serving, place your rice bowl close to them and gassho. But eat in moderation. Some teachers recommend that you eat only half or

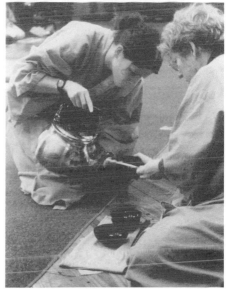

Oryoki. *After food has been served for oryoki, retreatants chant before beginning to eat (above). After the meal is finished, a small amount of water is added to rinse the bowl (right) so that no food is wasted.*

two-thirds as much food as you normally do. Moderation will leave you with greater clarity, not greater hunger. In any case, you must eat everything you are given, leaving nothing in your bowls. Hot water will be passed so that you can rinse your bowl; you may then drink the water or pour it into the vessel with the grains of rice for the hungry spirits.

The final act of mealtime is another chant—of gratitude for the food and of commitment to use the energy from it for the welfare of all beings.

DHARMA TALKS

During the afternoon session, the teacher usually gives a Dharma talk exploring various aspects of Zen teachings and practice. During this talk, you should continue to sit as you do for zazen, concentrating on the teacher's words as your focus.

At some zendos, the first Dharma talk covers aspects of meditation such as posture and breathing. Others may address key Zen topics such as the nature of Mind, emptiness, non-attachment, and enlightenment.

At the end of the Dharma talk, gassho in response to the teacher's bow, and wait until the teacher leaves the hall before you do.

WORK PERIODS

An important part of Zen practice is to be able to use the deeply meditative mind in physical or mental work. The work period *(samu)* during a sesshin is an excellent opportunity, in a controlled environment, for this practice. Samu as a monastic practice was established by the eighth-century master Pai-chang, who instituted it as an opportunity not only for practice but also for service to the Three Treasures: the Buddha, the Dharma, and the Sangha (see page 112). Pai-chang is credited with the familiar Zen saying that "A day without work is a day without food."

If you are relatively new to Zen, you are usually given some sort of physical work, such as cleaning kitchen fixtures, chopping vegetables, or weeding a garden, in which you can learn how to perform simple tasks mindfully. More experienced practitioners may be asked to work with a computer software problem or even to talk on the telephone without losing their meditative sesshin mind. Their challenge is to do more complex and potentially distracting tasks and be able to move directly back to a deep practice.

A critical aspect of sesshin, as of all of Zen, is the *sustained* effort to maintain mindfulness, no matter whether you

Samu. *During sesshin, work assignments such as raking or chopping vegetables let you bring mindfulness to the types of activities of your everyday life.*

are sitting in the zendo, walking in a courtyard, or scrubbing a pot. Samu gives you the chance to experience one-pointed concentration on the same kinds of tasks that will engage you when you go home and thus is a bridge to your life after the sesshin. You will learn that whether you are sitting in the formal setting of a zendo or on a folded pillow in the middle of your bed at home—or are sweeping a floor—you are at the gateway of liberation.

A word of caution: After you have attended a sesshin, reentry into the ordinary world may be quite startling. You may feel that you've "lost a layer" of your hide and are supersensitive to your surroundings. Be gentle with yourself. Give yourself time to settle back into your usual routine. Affirm your commitment to a daily practice to sustain the benefits you've gotten. And don't bother to try to explain what has happened to you to well-meaning friends who have no idea what you're talking about. There are a number of stories about trying to explain practice that usually end with an observation such as "My friends really resent me when I'm a Buddhist, but they love me when I'm a buddha." A counterpart to this statement is the irony of good news–bad news, succinctly observed by Zen scholar Albert Low in *Zen: Tradition and Transitions:* "The good news is that we are Buddha; the bad news is that *all* beings are Buddha. The sickness of being human is the sickness of wanting to be unique."

4

Mirrors of Practice

SANGHA AND

TEACHER

After the bell sounds, you bow to your companions and raise your eyes. Once again you're struck by what an unlikely assortment of people is sitting cross-legged on your living room rug. The first time you met together, people explained why they wanted to join a sitting group—most talked about relieving stress and finding that something was missing in their lives. You were the only one who mentioned Buddhism. Even that first time you all sat together, you felt a remarkable energy that seemed to soften and support you at the same time. You found yourself wanting to share that support with the others. No matter what had brought you together in the first place, over the months extraordinary bonds have formed as you have drawn strength from each other and recognized that you are all on the same path.

SANGHA

....

TO BECOME A pledged disciple of the Buddha, his first followers performed the simple ritual of repeating three times: "I take refuge in the Buddha; I take refuge in the Dharma; I take refuge in the Sangha." The Buddha (the historical figure known as Shakyamuni Buddha, the Buddha of the Shakya clan), the Dharma (the teachings of Shakyamuni Buddha), and the Sangha (the spiritual community of his immediate followers) have become known as the manifested Three Treasures, or Triple Jewel. At the Buddha's bidding, these monks, or *bhikkhus,* spent much of the year traveling and teaching his doctrines, but during each rainy season, when they gathered together for intensive meditation and study, they literally took refuge in the Sangha.

The first sangha was a particular group of monks, living under quite specific guidelines. Gradually, the concept of sangha expanded to include the nuns, novitiates, and lay practitioners who supported the monastic community. Today, especially in the West, the term *sangha* may be used for a small meditation group that meets in one's home, or for the people who regularly practice at a particular center, or for the worldwide community of all who follow the Buddha's teachings. But even in its most inclusive sense, the sangha today plays the same critical role that it did in the Buddha's time: It supports our continuing practice.

THE ROLE OF SANGHA

The role of sangha—in even the smallest group—is to keep us practicing. And why is this role necessary? It's a common occurrence to sit down, then decide that your time can best be used by doing something that you think of while you're sitting. It's even more common to feel that you're just too tired, too busy, or too distracted to take the time to sit at all. But if you've already said, "I'll see you at the zendo tonight," you'll go, even though you may not really feel like it, because you've made a commitment to the people in your sangha.

Just practicing together is the first level of being in a sangha. Something happens when more than one person is sitting. A kind of strength—a commonality—occurs. If one person is sleepy or is fidgety, it's as if he or she were being "held up" by the others who are sitting. It's a wonderful experience to be supported by and to support others in this way. In *Thousand Peaks*, Zen scholar Mu Soeng gives this colorful example of how a sangha works:

Together action is like washing potatoes. When people wash potatoes in Korea, instead of washing them one at a time, they put them all in a tub full of water. Then someone puts a stick in the tub and pushes it up and down, up and down. This makes the potatoes rub against each other; as they bump into each other, the hard crusty dirt falls off. If you wash potatoes one at a time, it takes a long time to clean each one, and only one potato gets clean at a time. If they are all together, the potatoes clean each other.

A sangha also offers the possibility of social action, in the broadest sense of being there for one another. If people get sick, you take care of them. You celebrate each other's birthdays. Even a very small sangha may go as a group to help out at a soup kitchen or a hospice. In general sanghas are involved in the same kinds of activities that you find in any ordinary Western congregation.

If your sangha is a Zen center, you will also be able to learn the more formal practices of Zen Buddhism by hearing Dharma talks and participating in services. The services are extraordinary opportunities for mindfulness, awareness, and reverence. Reverence, as expressed through formal elements of services such as bowing, is especially good for the ego and for ideas about who we are. It seems to be particularly difficult for Americans to bend themselves physically, psychically, and emotionally—to prostrate the highest part of themselves in the presence of others—but the discipline of expressing reverence can enhance the other aspects of your practice. And just as the earliest disciples became Buddhists through reciting the three Refuges, so today are Zen disciples initiated into Buddhism in the *jukai* ceremony by committing themselves to the Three Treasures and the Precepts (discussed in chapter 6), and the Four Vows (see page 136).

But how do you begin to look for a sangha, and how do you know if you have found the right one for you?

FINDING A SANGHA

How you go about finding a sangha will depend upon where you live. If you are in a major metropolitan area, your options will be quite different from those in a rural area. You can begin your search by reviewing the list of Zen centers in chapter 11; also, each issue of magazines such as *Tricycle* and *Shambhala Sun* carries listings. The Internet is another rich source of information on centers and sitting groups. In large cities, you can often find centers by looking up *Zen* in the telephone directory. If there is a Zen center nearby, you can begin there. If not, telephone the one closest to you to see if it has a listing for a sitting group near you. Find out when sittings take place, make plans to visit the centers or sitting groups in your area, and try them out.

You need to find a sangha that you can get to conveniently on a regular basis—*and* with people that you can get along with. You can tell in a few weeks if you have something in common with the people in a sangha, something that works for you. Sanghas have different "temperaments," depending on the individuals who make them up, and you shouldn't try to fit into a sangha if you are not compatible with its members. If you're uncomfortable after a few visits, try another sangha.

If you are isolated in a primarily rural region and there are no centers or sitting groups nearby, you probably will want to start a sitting group in your home town, perhaps after attending a sesshin or two at a center. The people who will want to sit with you may not be as homogeneous as a group would be in a big city, where there are many kinds of choices –you may have a yoga practitioner and someone in Vedanta along with a few people interested in Zen—but you all can have a rich experience sitting together.

The most successful small sitting groups are those that maintain consistency—as to when, where, and how they meet. The first time you come together, you may want to discuss as a group questions such as the time and length of the group sitting, whether you want to invite teachers or use audiotapes for Dharma talks at some of your sessions, the format in terms of sitting and walking, and whether you want to have "days of mindfulness" periodically.

Small sitting groups without teachers seem to benefit from

two other practices: attending, as a group, a sesshin at a center, and periodically taking stock of how the group is doing. The Vietnamese Zen teacher Thich Nhat Hanh has a valuable technique for such "group inventories," which he calls Watering the Flower. In this practice, the group sits in a circle (it's nice to have flowers in the center) for a few minutes. Then, in the first round, each person has the opportunity to express gratitude about some aspect of the sangha (for example, for a member's opening his or her home for sittings). At no time *must* anyone speak. In the second round, members may describe some way in which they could strengthen their own practice or some way, in the past, that they might have done more to strengthen the sangha (such as attending sittings more regularly). In the final round, each person has a chance to share about some way the sangha might be improved in the future (for example, making walking periods shorter or adding a potluck supper once a month). Then again the group sits together for a few minutes.

It's very important—even if you live at a distance from any center—to find a teacher that you like. If you've started a sitting group, it's fine to sit with only your sangha for a while, but if you are to practice Zen Buddhism, eventually you need to find a Zen teacher too.

ZEN TEACHERS

The relationship between teacher and student is one of the most special aspects of Zen Buddhism. In olden days, people used to go from mountain to mountain looking for a Zen teacher. Today you would go to several Zen centers to find someone with whom you feel you can work. But how do you know if you've found the right person? There are some helpful questions to ask yourself:

o Can I take risks with this teacher?
o Can I be a fool in front of this teacher?
o Can I say, "I don't know?" to this teacher?

If you can say *yes* to all these questions—can trust this teacher in these ways—then you've probably found a good teacher for you. If you can't answer *yes*, then you'll spend ten years just looking good.

SUPERFICIALLY, in American society, establishing a relationship with a teacher feels like a business transaction rather than a spiritual quest—you go someplace and perhaps become a member of a community so that you can practice with a particular teacher. But it's a much deeper relationship than it first appears to be. When a teacher takes a student on, the teacher is making a life commitment to serve that student, in all the ups and downs the student may go through. Awareness of this very powerful commitment is part of the training of teachers, and at different points along the path, the teacher and the student reaffirm their commitment to each other.

The teacher is there to nurture the student, to answer the student's questions, to prod the student—perhaps to make the student angry. The teacher will do whatever is necessary to help that student understand and experience the insight of wisdom. Japanese teacher Shundo Aoyama, in *Zen Seeds,* compares the teacher's role to lighting a candle:

On cold winter mornings, I sometimes find it hard to light a candle. I must slowly melt the wax surrounding the wick. The lit candle will then burn brightly and continue to burn, melting with the heat of its own light.

And so it is with human beings. At first, we must have a good teacher to guide us and "light us," but after that, by "burning ourselves" with our own efforts, we emit light and warmth around us. However earnestly someone else urges us to burn, unless we burn ourselves, nothing will be accomplished.

Sometimes, a student will find a very comfortable way to work with a teacher—then the teacher has to make that student uncomfortable. In other cases, the teacher's responsibility may be to support the student for years emotionally before the Dharma even comes up.

DOKUSAN

A very special experience within Zen is the private interview between teacher and student, or *dokusan*. This is the opportunity for you to ask questions about and get feedback on your practice confidentially. If you are a more advanced student working on a koan, it is the time for you to present your understanding of your koan to the teacher.

When a teacher has scheduled a period for dokusan, during zazen or at a sesshin, get in line with others waiting their turn, who often wait in a kneeling or cross-legged position outside the teacher's room. If prostrations are done at this zendo, you will do one prostration just inside the doorway when you enter, one in front of the teacher after you have approached within about two feet of him or her, and a third one at the doorway when you leave. After the second prostration, sit back on your heels in the seiza position, make eye contact with the teacher,

Dharma combat. *At Zen Mountain Monastery, senior students wait in line to do Dharma combat with Abbot John Daido Loori, whose introductory remarks have provided the seeds for the encounter.*

and state very simply what is happening in your practice. If you are counting breaths, you may say something like "I am counting breaths, but my mind seems to wander away by the time I get to *three*." Or you may have a question such as "How can I keep my attention on my breath rather than on the numbers when I am counting my breath?" The teacher may ask you a question— answer honestly and briefly—or may give you a suggestion. To end the dokusan, the teacher will ring a bell or say formal words such as "May your practice go well." You may also make a formal response, such as "Thank you for your teaching." Then you gassho, rise slowly, back toward the doorway, and do a final prostration.

Students may talk about their personal lives within the

context of the Dharma—because there's no real separation between personal life and Dharma. But one of the difficulties in American Zen is that students often slip into wanting psychological help. It's very tricky, but teachers must not be shrinks to their students. Teachers must always remind students that all we're looking for is a *spiritual* response. The teacher's formal question is: "How do you see that?" Because an interview with a student typically lasts five minutes or less, the interaction has a different pattern from therapy. It's a very elegant dance. It's as if two mirrors are facing one another.

If you study with a teacher for a long time, with both of you earnestly serving the Dharma, wonderful things can happen. Positions can change, and suddenly one day the teacher is the student and the student is the teacher. Incredible responsiveness occurs. The relationship between teacher and student is well expressed in a koan about a mother bird pecking from the outside of an egg and a baby bird pecking from the inside. Each is pecking away, trying to get rid of the eggshell. This image aptly reflects how a teacher and a student each work in their own way on the barriers to wisdom.

THE TITLE *TEACHER*

All lineages in Zen Buddhism try to ensure that people who have not been properly trained do not become teachers or have the title *teacher* attributed to them. For those who want to become teachers, each lineage has its own very precise series of steps, titles, and services that must be set up and documented, signed, and copied. The title *Zen teacher* means something. (For a discussion of other titles, see page 144.)

Ordination—the ceremonial induction into a specific Zen lineage as a monk or a nun—has nothing to do with being called a teacher. There are lay teachers and there are ordained teachers, and there are no differences between the two.

There are no classes in how to be a teacher: Zen students train one on one with their teacher. To be recognized as a Zen teacher, your teacher must recognize you. There's a process—usually at least ten years—during which the teacher notices the rough spots and helps to rub them off, before the student becomes a teacher. But the teacher does not *make* the student a teacher—just recognizes her or him. When the process is complete, there's a ceremony and the mind seal is transmitted, just as a koan describes the Buddha's transmission to Mahakashyapa, considered the first ancestor of Zen Buddhism. In this koan, the Buddha was sitting before his disciples. Suddenly, he picked up a flower and twirled it. Mahakashyapa smiled, and the Buddha said, "I have the treasury of the eye of the true Dharma and wondrous mind of nirvana, and I transmit it to Mahakashyapa." This koan is about the mind-to-mind transmission of the Dharma from one teacher to the next. Mahakashyapa responded to the Buddha's action, and the Buddha acknowledged that. Was anything handed from one person to the next? Or was there a recognition?

MUTUAL RESPECT

There is some tricky territory in the relationship with a teacher. In order to benefit from the teacher-student relationship, it is important for the student to be open and to trust the teacher. Most teachers are skillful with this trust, opening a mutual ground that allows them to challenge students' fixed ideas about practice and enlightenment. Unless the student trusts the teacher, these challenges will not serve their purpose.

On the other hand, teachers, being human, can be susceptible to the idealization of their students and thus abuse their "power." This dynamic exists in all spiritual traditions, and Zen is no exception. It is good to remember that a student can trust and appreciate the teacher *and* maintain a balanced view of the relationship.

WHEN YOU BEGIN to seek a teacher, it's very important to have a "beginner's mind" and not cling to old ideas of what a Zen teacher looks like or how a Zen teacher acts or how a Zen teacher should be. Just try to have an open mind. The experience is illustrated by a marvelous koan called "Joshu's Bridge." Joshu (Chao-chou) was the great teacher of Tang dynasty China, and what he said was so wonderful that light was said to sparkle from his mouth when he spoke. He lived on a mountain that had a stone bridge known for its beauty all over China. Once a cocky young monk came to visit him and called out, "I came to see the stone bridge of Joshu, but all I see here is a wooden bridge." Joshu looked at him steadily and said, "You see only a wooden bridge? Well, it lets horses cross. It lets asses cross. Come on over." What students see is what students get. No matter where students are, here's the teacher to meet them—right here, ready to serve, whether the teacher is serving an ass or a horse.

5

Roots That Support and Nourish

A BRIEF HISTORY

OF ZEN BUDDHISM

The diffused winter light casts few shadows on the small altar you've set up where you meditate. One. Two. Barely have you begun to count your breaths when the pain in your knee starts. Your left knee. It's always your left knee. You wonder how long the pain will last this time. You try to ignore it, then to will it away. Then you bargain with it: If you don't go away by the time I reach ten, I'll move. One. Two. Three . . . When your head bounces, your realize that the pain is gone but you've been dozing. "How long have I been out of it?" you wonder. Then your thoughts take off: "I can't be late for work this morning because I've got to do that presentation, and I have to iron my shirt, and the car needs gas. Perhaps I should just get up now— with so much to do, I'm just wasting my time sitting here trying to count my breath." This morning—as you do each time you sit and confront the machinations of your mind—you have reenacted the Buddha's enlightenment experience. One.

EACH TIME WE MEDITATE, whether we consciously think of it or not, we are participating in the Buddha's life. Maezumi Roshi, the Japanese teacher who founded the Zen Center of Los Angeles, once commented that in Japan, everyone knows the life of the Buddha, so a Zen practitioner there would not have to study it—this knowledge is part of the culture. But in the United States, many Zen teachers are beginning to recognize that a lack of attention to the life of the Buddha is a deficiency in our appreciation of the Dharma as a whole. Zen students need to understand that the roots—what's underneath the practice—are what support and nourish Zen Buddhism. When we look at the story of the Buddha's life, we find in every phrase some kind of teaching point that has been used in one tradition or another during the teachings' 2,500-year journey from northern India to the United States.

PARTICIPATING IN THE BUDDHA'S LIFE

There is no one source of historical details of the Buddha's life. Much of what we know about him was communicated orally for several centuries after his death and was finally written down as part of his discourses, or sutras. There were also literary records, such as Ashvaghosha's first-century epic poem, the *Buddha-charita* ("Life of the Buddha"), that were filled with the stuff of cult myths. Many of these legendary stories tell of events such as his mother's conceiving him when she dreamed that a white elephant's tusk pierced her side, or of how, immediately after his birth, the child stood up, took seven steps (where immediately lotuses bloomed), raised a hand to heaven, and announced that he would achieve nirvana. Nevertheless, some elements of his life story seem fairly consistent across a number of sources and are important for students of Zen.

The historical Buddha was probably born during the sixth century B.C.E. into a family of rulers of the Shakya clan, a warrior class, in what is now Nepal. (Although 563–483 B.C.E. are his most generally accepted life dates, current research indicates that he may have been born considerably later and may have died as recently as 400 B.C.E.) Before he was born, a seer predicted that he would become either a great ruler or a great religious teacher. His father, Suddhodana, knowing that the life of a spiritual teacher was one of renunciation and wanting his heir to rule after him, raised his child in such a way that he would not be inclined to pursue spiritual matters but rather would take on the rulership of the clan and their kingdom. Suddhodana reasoned that the best way to ensure this path was to provide every manner of comfort for his son, named Siddhartha Gautama, to keep him from any contact or involvement with society, and to protect him from suffering. This desire to protect Siddhartha from suffering is an important element, from a Zen Buddhist point of view, because what leads so many people to a spiritual journey—and to Zen practice—is the *apprehension* of suffering, whether it is our own or that of others. That's the itch that gets us on the spiritual path.

The old texts tell us that Siddhartha was raised inside the palace walls, isolated from everything beyond the three palaces—one for each season—that Suddhodana built for his comfort. So "censored" was his exposure to the world, it is said, that his father had all dead flowers plucked from the trees on the route before Siddhartha went from one palace to another. Despite being pampered with sense pleasures, he grew into a beautiful young man spiritually, intellectually, and physically. He married an equally kind and attractive woman, Yashodhara —some accounts say his father chose her, as was the custom, but others detail his winning her in martial-arts contests—and they had a son, named Rahula.

Siddhartha had everything he wanted, but nevertheless he was curious about what was going on in the outside world. On four different nights, he sneaked out of the palace with his charioteer, and each night he had a significant and traumatic encounter with the human drama. The first night, he saw someone who was quite old. When he asked about the man, his charioteer told him that all of us eventually grow old and bent over, like the person Siddhartha saw. The next night, Siddhartha saw a man who was very ill and was lying in the road. He asked about that man too and learned that all of us are subject to disease and physical suffering. He saw a corpse on the following night and discovered that all who are born grow old and eventually die. In these three nights, Siddhartha encountered illness, old age, and death—essential elements of the human condition to which even Siddhartha himself was heir. Later, in his first teaching, he identified these three as primary factors in the suffering that is the common experience of all people.

On the fourth night that Siddhartha went outside the palace, what he found was a *sadhu,* a wandering ascetic on a spiritual path. Despite the sadhu's rags, there was a calmness and peacefulness about him that was very appealing to Siddhartha. When Siddhartha asked about the ascetic, his charioteer explained that the man was on a spiritual quest, seeking the answer to the mysteries of life and death, of suffering. That response is an essential point, because the Buddha himself spent the next six years searching for those answers, and his first teaching, the Four Noble Truths, addressed suffering.

For Zen practitioners, another important aspect of the Buddha's life was that after discovering the facts of old age, illness, and death, he gave up—*renounced*—some of the things in his life. In this case, he left his palace, his wife, and his son in order to seek enlightenment. In some versions of his story, a grief-stricken Siddhartha stole away from his family in the middle of the night after looking in on his sleeping wife and child. The earliest discourses indicate, however, that his family knew of his decision and that his tearful father watched him go. In either case, the renunciation aspect of the story reflects what would have been emphasized to his early followers—a group of monks—but we can take it symbolically and say that each one of us gives up something. We do so to meditate. We do so to be mindful and aware. And we do have to give up other aspects of our lives when we make a decision to live according to the Eightfold Path (page 108). It doesn't mean that we have to stop nourishing ourselves or lead a monastic existence. It does mean that there is a certain element of letting go—of habits of mind, of relationships that aren't healthy—when we enter upon a spiritual path.

It's important to note that after Siddhartha left the palace, it took him six years of searching to find his answer. He wandered throughout northern India, seeking the most respected sages of his day. He embraced several well-known paths and actually became a leader in two different traditions, whose teachers proclaimed that he had attained the highest level of spiritual achievement. But he left both of them and continued his search because he knew that although he had achieved the highest levels of meditative absorption, those practices had not answered *his* question. This part of the Buddha's story is especially important for us because it emphasizes both his own individual awareness and how much of the path is filled with hardship. Eventually, he let go of the very severe ascetic practices, just as he had let go of a life of luxury, and chose what is known as the Middle Way. The Middle Way is not an exotic or intoxicating path but is simply a balance of mind and of body in the daily life that we lead—a very different approach in the Buddha's time, and one that is significant for Zen practitioners today. The lesson for us is that the spiritual path exists within our life itself—it's not just something we do on a retreat or a visit to Asia.

When Siddhartha accepted that the path is the Middle Way, he sat down and said, "I will not get up until I see into the nature of the unborn mind." That declaration is significant for our practice because that's what we do every time we sit down on a cushion to meditate. We say, "I am going to penetrate into the mystery of who I am, into my true nature." It's something Siddhartha did alone, by himself, sitting on a cushion of grasses under a bodhi (fig) tree near the village of Bodhgaya in northern India. We think of ourselves, when we sit down to meditate, as being the Buddha and the Buddha as us, and we become the Awakened One each time. Meditation—zazen—is the heart of Zen practice, the heart of the Zen tradition. That moment when Siddhartha sat down for the first time is thus the heart of the teaching of the Buddha's life for us as Zen practitioners.

As Siddhartha sat, he entered increasingly deeper meditative states. In the so-called first watch of the night, from dusk to ten P.M., he had cognition of his thousands of past lives. During the second watch, from ten P.M. to two A.M., he came to understand the functioning of cause and effect, of karma. During the third watch, from two A.M. to dawn, he had cognition of the interdependence of all things, the nature of suffering, and the end of suffering. At dawn he was liberated, enlightened, awakened, the Buddha.

There are many stories of the Buddha's temptations during that night as he sat meditating. They tell of the same temptations that assail us when we meditate: sexual desire, aversion to unpleasantness, hunger for possessions and pleasant experiences, and doubt. A being called Mara, who may be seen as the manifestation of our minds, is said to have challenged the Buddha with the question "Who are you?"—the same question that stops so many practitioners and causes them to lose confidence in their own ability. Who am I to practice? I'm me. I practice. This is it—I sit down and practice and trust that experience. To derive comfort from our practice is important, and

Buddha in the Bhumisparsha mudra.
The Buddha touched the earth with his right hand during the night of his enlightenment, invoking the earth's affirmation of his experience in the face of taunts by Mara.

the Buddha, seeing the destructiveness of doubt, invoked the earth itself as the witness to his right to practice. This moment of the enlightenment is frequently depicted in statues of the Buddha, who, sitting in a meditative posture on a lotus pedestal, reaches down with his right hand to touch the earth.

After his enlightenment, the Buddha spent about seven weeks near Bodhgaya. The accounts we have say that at first he did not intend to share what he had learned, convinced that people could not understand his teachings, the Dharma. But his compassion for all beings soon led him—some stories say after the intervention of a god—to begin walking toward Benares (Sarnath), 130 miles away, to teach. Along the way, he encountered five ascetics with whom he had practiced at one time. When they saw him, at first they rejected him because he clearly no longer followed their ascetic practices, which had left him emaciated and weak before he embraced the Middle Way. But there was something so radiant about him that they were drawn to him despite themselves and became his first disciples. When they reached Benares, they went together into the Deer Park there, and the newly enlightened Buddha gave his first sermon: the Four Noble Truths of suffering, the origination of suffering, the end of suffering, and the path to the end of suffering, discussed fully in chapter 6.

The rest of the Buddha's life was one of service and of putting together a set of codes for his followers. It was always clear that the guidelines he expressed were flexible—there are many stories of how his senior disciples nagged him about the "rules" for the monks. He didn't mind. They walked around northern India together serving and teaching. And this is a critical point: Each one of us can have a life of service, whether we ordain or live a householder's life with our families—we can live a life of service to our community regardless of what kind of work we do. The lesson is that to serve is to fully participate in the Buddha's life.

A wonderful way to think of the Buddha is the way he thought of himself: as an educator, in the best sense of one who enables us to learn. The word *teacher* implies student, implies someone who is open to learning. A master commands. A guru leads. But a teacher offers an activity that is really on the student's behalf and invites the student to participate in the teachings. The Buddha repeatedly stressed, "Be a light unto yourselves." So we call the Dharma the teachings—not the commandments—a choice of words that reflects the extraordinary self-empowerment that is so basic to the Buddha's teaching.

After teaching for about forty years, the Buddha passed away, or entered *Parinirvana* ("extinction," or final release from *samsara*), near Kushinagara, after eating poisoned pork or mushrooms, according to stories of the time. As he was dying, he called together his disciples and offered to answer any last questions, but none was asked. His final words were: "Impermanent are all created things. Strive on mindfully." If we take nothing else from his teachings, these two sentences, embracing reality and encouragement, can carry our practice, as they have supported others' for more than 2,500 years.

REVOLUTIONARY TEACHINGS

Although we shall look closely at some of the Buddha's major teachings from a Zen perspective in chapter 6, it is important to recognize here that in some critical ways his teachings were revolutionary at the time he gave them.

The Buddha was the only founder of a major religion who claimed to be neither a god nor a messenger of a god. In many ways his teachings were similar to those of his day and used some of the same vocabulary, but some of his convictions differed dramatically from the tenets of the most common religions surrounding him. In the Buddha's teachings, for example, there was an absence of theism, or belief in gods; animal sacrifice was forbidden; and his community did not recognize a caste system—even untouchables became part of his sangha. But there were two other revolutionary differences that have had great impact on Buddhism as a whole since its beginning: in function, the absence of a priestly class of intermediaries; and in concept, the teaching of no self.

During the Buddha's time, the major religions had *Brahmans*—a strong priestly class who were the interpreters between gods and the people. The Buddha ordained people, but the members of his sangha were not intermediaries between a divinity and the people. Rather, each person—ordained or not—had the opportunity to learn from the Buddha's teachings and to become enlightened, or awake. Today each person's potential for enlightenment is an intrinsic Zen teaching.

The concept of *Anatman* ("no self") was contrary to the religions of his day, all of which centered on *Atman*, a permanent, unchanging soul (see page 124). When he referred to no self, the Buddha meant that each of us has no separate, independent, eternal self. He didn't mean that we don't have a particular style and way of being—which is impermanent and constantly changing. Buddhism doesn't make everything homogeneous; it recognizes all kinds of beings. It honors diversity. To understand no self is to understand an aspect of consciousness in which we are one with all beings Still, we stand on our own two feet.

With the lesson of his life and these religious innovations in mind, let's see now what happened to his teachings as they were spread around the world.

THE 2,500-YEAR JOURNEY

A most powerful and beautiful aspect of Buddhism is how it has taken the shape of the container that has held it in each place it has settled. A bowl can be narrow and tall or wide and short, simple or ornate, yet hold its contents well. Inevitably, Buddhism has also changed the vessel, and this transformation was no more evident than when Buddhism reached China and spread to Japan, Korea, and Vietnam. The practices of Buddhism as they existed in India and were transmitted southward to countries like Sri Lanka and Thailand probably resemble their origins more closely today than they do in the countries of the northern transmission.

BUDDHISM IN INDIA

Siddhartha Gautama was born into, was raised within, and sought enlightenment through the religions of his day in northern India. Many of his teachings were generally within those traditions, with a few important exceptions. During the Buddha's lifetime, he articulated two major types of statements (sutras): the Dharma, or teachings or doctrine; and the Vinaya, codified rules of conduct for monks that grew out of their experiences in the first sangha. Both were maintained through oral tradition, with monks reciting sutras in unison daily—in this way, if one made a mistake, the group as a whole did not change the teachings. In fact, there were written languages at the time, but the Sangha mistrusted the accuracy of what one person might record. The first written version of the teachings is believed to have taken place in Sri Lanka when an epidemic struck a monastery and the monks were afraid that they all would die—and the teachings would be lost if they didn't write them down. This body of teachings was the so-called *Pali canon*, written in Pali, a language predating and similar to Sanskrit, in which many later versions of the teachings were recorded. The practice of oral transmission accounts for the repetition and some of the other stylistic patterns that made the sutras easier to memorize.

Before the Buddha's death, he is said to have told his attendant, Ananda, that some of the Vinaya rules could be modified in the future, but unfortunately, he did not say specifically which ones. As a result of this absence of clear directions, there have been challenges that have affected Buddhism throughout its history. The first disputes seem to have broken out within a month of the Buddha's passing, and his senior disciple, Mahakashyapa, to whom he had transmitted the mind seal (see page 73), called what is known as the First Council. At this gathering of five hundred senior disciples, Ananda recited all the Dharma teachings, and another disciple, Upali, recited the Vinaya. All these recitations were accepted by the council as the Buddha's authentic teachings and are the foundation of the teachings that have come down to us, especially in the Theravada tradition.

About a hundred years later, another dispute arose—primarily about the prohibition against monks' handling money—

and the Second Council reaffirmed the Vinaya. As a result, several sects split off, including one known as Mahasangha (the "Great Sangha"), which was probably a forerunner of Mahayana and therefore Zen Buddhism. Two more councils were held: About two hundred years after the Buddha's passing, the third was convened by Ashoka, who essentially made India a Buddhist empire and spread Buddhism southward to Southeast Asia; and in about 100 C.E., King Kanishka called the fourth. Many changes were taking place in society between 100 B.C.E. and 100 C.E. Among the most important were, first, the shift to a written language and thus the creation of written collections of the Dharma, with the introduction of new materials, and, second, the fragmentation of Buddhist sects.

Buddhism was a major force in India for a thousand years after the Buddha lived there. Over time, however, it weakened through the fragmentation of sects despite the fact that they lived closely together, the reascendancy of theistic religions such as Hinduism, and the incursion of invaders. Of those who entered India, the Muslims were the most powerful and the most adamant about replacing local beliefs with the teachings of Islam. By the thirteenth century, Buddhism no longer flourished in the land where it had been born. It existed in Southeast Asia, where it had been taken by Ashoka and where Theravada Buddhists are still the majority in some countries, and in the north. It was through the northern transmission that Zen has come to us.

INDIA TO CHINA

When Buddhism was at its peak in India, its character was immediately identifiable in the sutras composed there. They are filled with numbers and mathematical formulas; they have

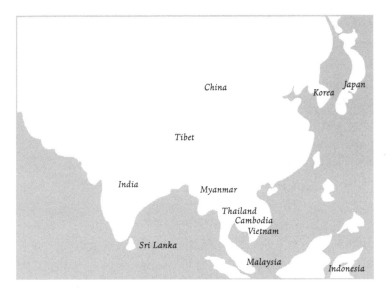

The spread of Buddhism. *In the southern transmission, Buddhism spread from India to what is now Sri Lanka (Ceylon), Myanmar (Burma), Thailand, Kampuchea (Cambodia), and Indonesia. In the northern transmission, Buddhism spread into central Asia, China, Tibet, Korea, and Japan.*

beautifully intricate numerical concepts interwoven with symbolic ideas; and they are heavily wrought with wonderful questionings of logic and cosmology. That's what you find when Buddhism is in its magnificent Indian container.

And when Buddhism flowed into China, it got a real taste of the earth. A kind of ordinariness greatly influenced by Taoism came over Buddhism, particularly the outgrowth that became Zen (*Ch'an* in China). Buddhist teachings had come into China piecemeal for many centuries, carried at first by travelers along the Silk Route, from central Asia across China. By the sixth century C.E., there were many Buddhist sects, Buddhism had entered the mainstream of court life, and the thousands of monasteries and convents were under govern-ment control.

Ch'an was the most enduring of the Chinese sects, and its characteristics—and therefore Zen's—were primarily deter-mined by the arrival in the sixth century of the legendary fig-ure Bodhidharma. This Indian master, depicted in paintings as a glowering man who cut off his eyelids to stay awake during meditation, is said to have arrived in 520 C.E., to have had an unpleasant encounter with Emperor Wu of Liang (reputedly a Buddhist devotee who built many temples throughout his realm), then to have spent the next nine years meditating while facing a wall in the Shaolin temple. Stories about Bodhidharma abound, including one of a young man who sought to be his disciple and cut off his arm with a sword to prove his sincerity; Bodhidharma accepted him. Bodhidharma is recognized as the First Ancestor, or Patriarch, of Ch'an/Zen, following direct transmission of the Dharma through twenty-seven masters, beginning with the Buddha, then Mahakashyapa.

Through centuries of political and social upheaval in China, two Buddhist schools founded in the mid-ninth century survived and became foundations of the strongest Zen sects in Japan and the West today: *Lin-chi,* which is Japanese Rinzai, and *Ts'ao-tung,* which in Japan is Soto. During this period, Buddhism was spread rapidly and widely by the invention by Buddhist monks of the printing process; the earliest printed book that still exists today is a version of *The Diamond Sutra* from 868. Chinese Buddhists, too, in the twelfth century originated the ten *Oxherding Pictures,* probably the most well known and inspi-rational visual expression of Zen worldwide (see page 129).

The vessel that became Zen was shaped in China by the Taoist understanding of simplicity and harmony with nature, as well as the value of everyday life. The profound *Faith-Mind Sutra*—beginning "The great way is not difficult; simply avoid picking and choosing"—reads like a Taoist text. But it's a sixth-century Buddhist text, from the Third Ancestor, Seng t'san (Sosan in Japanese), who was a leper. Zen as we know it was most deeply affected in China by Hui-neng (E'no in Japanese), an illiterate woodcutter who became the Sixth Ancestor. He fully understood that "Be a lamp unto yourself," for a Chinese Zen Buddhist, meant adding the teachings of Taoism to the bowl. Work and such simple everyday acts as planting one's own garden were seen as having great value. Pai-chang, the eighth-century abbot of a large monastery who insisted that a day without work was a day without food, practiced what he preached. When he got to be quite old and frail, monks in his monastery hid his gardening tools in an effort to stop him from exhausting himself. He stopped eating until the tools were restored to him.

In China, unlike India, it was not easy to be a mendicant, going from place to place, begging for food and teaching. When large monasteries were established, the monks could not be supported by the communities, as they had been in India, so there was a need for them to work, to support themselves, and the monks began to farm. This great influx of the Taoist spirit—of being one with the earth, taking from the earth, working the earth, using our daily life as our practice—had an enormous influence on the countryside and the community and is central to the Zen tradition.

At the same time, elements of Confucianism also entered the Zen bowl of Buddhism. The great respect for ancestry found in Zen, as well as aspects of etiquette and form, come out of Confucian ancestor worship and respect for the elders. The

Confucian influence was most strongly felt when Zen Buddhism flowed from the eastern Chinese bowl to a beautiful lacquer bowl in Japan.

After periods of growth and strength and decline and weakness, both the Chinese empire and Buddhism were deteriorating by the beginning of the twentieth century. Finally, the Communist Cultural Revolution of 1965–1975 destroyed many manifestations of "culture," including Buddhist monasteries, convents, and artifacts. In recent years, the Communist government has somewhat relaxed its stranglehold on religion, but none of the Buddhist sects have regained much of the popularity they once had. Nevertheless, China was the main conduit for Buddhism's spread to other cultures in Asia—especially Vietnam, Korea, and Japan, where their national brands of Zen still flourish.

CHINA AND INDIA TO VIETNAM

The land now known as Vietnam, a finger-shaped country in Indochina along the South China Sea, has been subject to incursions of many sorts throughout its history. Writing, literature, political practices, religion, and armies came, entered, and conquered—for a while. In the southern part of the country, the Indian influence, including Theravada Buddhism, was pervasive until the fifteenth century, when powerful northern people, heavily affected by Chinese culture, began to dominate it.

The Chinese influence in northern Vietnam had begun in ancient times, when that area was considered little more than a Chinese province. During the Tang dynasty in China (581–907), rulers united China and promoted throughout their country and their empire a form of Buddhism/Confucianism that was widespread in Vietnam until that country achieved independence in the tenth century. Although several Chinese schools of Buddhism took hold in Vietnam, *Thien*—Vietnam's version of Ch'an—has been the strongest. Despite protracted civil conflict and disastrous wars involving France and the United States, Vietnamese Buddhism has waned but has not been extinguished. Today an estimated 80 percent of the population is Buddhist.

The Thien monk Thich Nhat Hanh, who lives in exile in France, has gained worldwide attention as an advocate of "engaged Buddhism" (see chapter 9) and has become a model of social action for Zen Buddhists.

CHINA TO KOREA

The Vietnamese vessel for Buddhism is relatively small, a factor that discourages fragmentation and encourages nationalism. The effects of size caused a similar adhesion when Buddhism flowed into the Korean peninsula. But part of the fabric of this container was a native shamanistic religion that gave Buddhism a distinctly Korean quality. Buddhist temples were often built on mountaintops to pay homage to native spirits who lived there in the form of tigers and to enlist their fierce power for the benefit of the kingdom.

Buddhism was brought from China into the three kingdoms of Korea during the fourth century C.E. Korea was unified in the seventh century, and many new elements of Chinese culture were absorbed, including arts, political philosophy, and religion.

Ch'an is believed to have been brought to Korea in about 630 C.E. by a monk who had studied in China, but *Son,* as it was called, encountered doctrinal challenges that nearly suppressed it, despite the fact that Buddhism continued as the national religion. Not until Son master Chinul founded his *Chogye* order in the late twelfth century did Son fully take the shape it would have into the present.

Political and military invasions have affected Buddhism in Korea in the centuries since Chinul. Japan annexed Korea in 1910 and during its thirty-year rule exerted great pressure on Son to change some of its basic practices, such as celibacy among monastics. In 1948 the country was divided into two republics, North and South Korea, which soon were at war. Since the end of the war, in 1953, little has been known about Buddhism in the country that is North Korea. In the south, Son is widely practiced and encouraged, and several leading Chogye masters—especially Seung Sahn, founder of the *Kwan Um school*—have taught extensively and founded many centers in the West.

CHINA TO JAPAN

When Zen Buddhism came to Japan from China and Korea, it acquired all the refinements and formal elements associated with Japanese culture. The Zen Buddhist tradition became very involved with and was always associated with the arts in Japan. There was an interrelationship of the arts influencing Zen practice and Zen practice shaping the arts, seen clearly in the tea ceremony and calligraphy, which in their spontaneity and appreciation of the ordinary show both formalism and a reaction to formalism. This interrelationship with the arts in Zen's early days in Japan has continued throughout its history, and many artists have been attracted to Zen because of it.

The Japanese emphasis on form and refinement produced a paradoxical effect on Buddhism: There was a kind of spontaneous breaking away from the standards and rituals of Buddhist practice and at the same time an observance of them. This observance reached its culmination in Japan. With each bow and gesture mindfully choreographed and with altars and robes impeccably presented, the formalization and refinement of ritual and practice revealed a beautiful, elegant, and subtle norm. In the midst of this very formal tradition, Zen Buddhists like the seventeenth-century master Bankei, who were opposed to Zen's having a particular form, wandered from one place to another simply urging people to realize the unborn mind and insisting that nothing else—bows, services, meditation—is called for. The seemingly contradictory presence of formal elements and spontaneity that arose in Japan is still characteristic of Zen today.

Before Buddhism arrived in Japan, the dominant religion was worship of *kami,* powerful indigenous spirits, often found in trees, waterfalls, and other natural phenomena. Buddhism was brought to Japan in the sixth century by immigrants and visiting political delegations from Korea. At first there was some transference, with Buddha images being treated as kami, and disputes arose between those who held to the older beliefs and adherents of Buddhism. Prince Shotoku (573–622) is credited with founding Buddhism and writing into the first constitution guidelines for belief—in kamism, Buddhism, and Confucianism, which was also an important system for social position and duty. At this point, first through Korea, then directly from China, many aspects of Chinese culture were imported into Japan, including a writing system, government systems, and religious sects. The strong link between religion and the imperial court led to cycles of corruption and reactionarily strict monastic practices.

The Kamakura era (1185–1333) was a period of political, social, cultural, and religious upheaval. Warriors known as shoguns effectively took power from the emperor and instituted many changes. Buddhism now became accessible to laypeople, not just courtiers, and many new sects arose. Two sects important to the future of Buddhism came into Japan from China during this period. Eisai introduced the (Rinzai) Oryo lineage in the late twelfth century and founded the first Rinzai (Chinese Lin-chi) monastery in Japan, and Dogen (1200–1253) brought the Soto (Chinese Ts'ao-tung) tradition in the early thirteenth century. In the ensuing eight or nine hundred years that Zen has been in Japan, although other groups have formed and broken away, essentially these have been the two large institutions of Zen Buddhism in that country, and they represent two of the contradictory impulses of Zen.

In the Soto tradition, there is a great reverence for form and an emphasis on silent illumination—on shikantaza, or just sitting—the practice of "sitting mind," of just sitting and allowing whatever comes up to come up and to fall away. In the Rinzai tradition, there is a strong impulse to study koans and a much more vigorous and active style within the monasteries—physical activity, raised voices, and questions and answers. It's a little less soft, a little more aggressive. At least, that is the way these traditions have always been described, but in the last ten years new material coming out of Japan indicates that the distinctions were never so clear-cut and that there have always been overlaps between the two traditions. Anytime a Zen teacher in the Soto tradition felt as though his group was getting too sleepy, he had no problem using techniques from the Rinzai tradition.

And in the Rinzai tradition, if people were too loud and active and were not really meditating, then the teacher would bring in techniques from the Soto tradition.

It's important for our understanding of Zen in America that we recognize these overlaps in traditions—and in individual students. The usual description of Japanese traditions sounds like a polarity, a splitting, in which a student has to like one or the other. But in fact they are two impulses during meditation that can exist in any one person. We can each have the impulse to sit quietly and the impulse to actively pursue an answer. The balancing of those impulses became unmistakable when Japanese Buddhism flowed into the American mixing bowl.

JAPAN TO THE UNITED STATES

Zen Buddhism came into the United States first as an import, with all the trappings of the East. Although many people date its arrival to Soyen Shaku's appearance at the World Parliament of Religions in Chicago in 1893, interest in Zen really took hold with the popularity of D. T. Suzuki's writings in the late 1940s and early 1950s. Initially, much of what was being written about Buddhism set out to make clear the difference between Western religious thought and Eastern thought. Today, this kind of dichotomy is not very useful. The Zen way of thinking (or "Zen mind") *has* come in from Eastern religions and philosophies. But it has also come in from science and ecology and a mixing of other theories and philosophies during the last fifty years, so it's no longer particularly beneficial to signify that Buddhism is an Eastern commodity. Buddhism here has already become thoroughly American. At the same time, we have not lost the essential teachings. We have not lost the understanding of suffering as an element in life, the understanding of the impermanence of all things, and the concept of no separate self.

Buddhism in America is a melange of a great many influences. Perhaps three of the greatest have been feminism, psychology, and lay practice. There is no question about the enormous impact that feminism has had on Buddhism in this country. Just at the time that Buddhism was forming here, feminism arose as an expression of the desire to have nonpatriarchal, nonhierarchical organizations, as a way to question authority, and as a way to question difference in a community. Quite naturally, feminism swirled into the mix of Zen Buddhism. Not just issues like the numbers of female and male teachers were affected. Rather, the very forms that Zen Buddhist organizations and the power structures have taken in this country have been informed by feminist practice, and women have attained the highest positions in Zen communities. Jiyu Kennett Roshi, who died in 1996, was the first woman who founded and became abbot of a Zen monastery—now called Shasta Abbey, in California. Today, many ordained women are senior heads of Zen centers, including Blanche Hartman at the Zen Center of San Francisco; Karen Sunna at the Minnesota Zen Meditation Center; Katherine Thanas at Santa Cruz Zen Center; Yvonne Rand at Redwood Creek Zen Center (in California); Charlotte Joko Beck at Zen Center of San Diego; Jisho Warner at Stone Creek Zendo (in California); Pat Enkyo O'Hara at the Village Zendo (in New York); and Bonnie Myotai Treace at the Zen Center of New York City.

Another factor is that the United States is a very "psychological" country and uses psychology as a kind of religion. The Zen Buddhist teachings of meditation and of one's experience with reality could be and have been easily interpreted within a

Although we usually hear of Zen coming to the West from the East, here we see Jisho Warner of Stone Creek Zendo, Sebastopol, California, at Eiheiji, the head temple-monastery of Soto Zen in Japan, October 1998, performing zuise. In this traditional ceremony, a priest pays homage to the school's founders and becomes honorary abbot of Eiheiji and officiant for a day.

psychological framework, and the understanding of psychological principles has in fact enriched Zen practice. Today, psychology is so entwined with some people's practice that they cannot separate them. You hear people say, "I don't want to be spiritual. I just want to practice Zen in order to get my life together." They don't realize that spirituality *is* getting your life together.

Finally, lay practice has had great influence here. The Buddhism that came from Japan was primarily a Zen Buddhism of ordained monks and priests who were supported by large communities. In this country, there has arisen a strictly American way of organizing Zen centers: usually a group of lay practitioners who run or are on the boards of directors of these communities—these nonprofit corporations. Lay practice is active, involved practice, not just a matter of financial support, and lay practitioners meditate and take leading practice roles in most centers.

These three factors have contributed to an American Zen Buddhism that looks very different from the one that arrived from Japan. Although here we've been looking primarily at a very Japan-centric kind of Zen Buddhism, other cultures have also been shaping Zen Buddhism to their needs and have fed into the American experience. The cultural flavorings are particularly evident in the teachings of contemporary Zen masters such as Sheng-Yen from China, Thich Nhat Hanh from Vietnam, and Seung Sunim from Korea. It is impossible, for example, to separate the teachings of Thich Nhat Hanh—who was nominated by Martin Luther King, Jr., for the Nobel Peace Prize—from the experience of Vietnam in the 1960s and 1970s. He and his culture were formed by the French influence—and the prolonged war—in Vietnam.

These different cultural influences have shaped the way we experience Zen, but at the same time, as we'll see in the coming chapters, the fundamental Zen experience of enlightenment, of no-self, doesn't change. It just looks different.

6

Stepping into Ourselves

BASIC ZEN

TEACHINGS

You came to the Zen center because you wanted to meditate—that's all. There was something missing in your life, and you thought that meditation would help to fill that void and make you more peaceful. But hardly have you begun to sit than you encounter a formidable presence: your own mind. You wonder what you've gotten yourself into.

DOGEN, THE THIRTEENTH-CENTURY founder of the Soto Zen tradition, remarked:

> To study the Way is to study the self.
> To study the self is to forget the self.
> To forget the self is to be enlightened by the
>   ten thousand things.

An essential teaching of Zen Buddhism is that when we start out on the path, we're stepping into ourselves. We're stepping into studying the ways to study the self. As we begin to shine the light of questioning upon ourselves—as we begin to meditate and experience concentration and mindfulness—we discover that the Way is not outside us, that to study is to begin where we are, with each breath: "To study the Way is to study the self."

The next line—"To study the self is to forget the self"—is where we become aware of the five *skandhas,* or aggregates, that constitute our being: corporeality, or form; sensation; perception; mental formations, or thoughts; and consciousness. For example, what happens when you are doing zazen at a sesshin and you hear a bell ring twice? A *corporeal* organ, the ear, receives the *sensation* of sound waves; because you are *conscious,* you *perceive* the sound waves as a bell ringing, and you *remember* that two rings mean that it's time to rise and begin kinhin.

In Buddhism the five skandhas are believed to constitute the totality that most people think of as the personality or the individual. None of the five can exist without the others—to rise after the bell sounds, you must have ears, be conscious so that you can experience sensation and perception, and mentally know what the other four experiences mean.

Further—and this is important—each of the skandhas is a source of attachment and therefore suffering, and all are impermanent. Think about another example: eating. When your tongue touches the first bite, a chemical reaction triggers the complex sensations that make up taste, which you perceive and recognize as ice cream. And you want another bite. If the ice cream had not touched your tongue, or if you had not tasted it, or had not recognized it, or had not thought of ice cream, you would not be longing for more. Also, if you filled your mouth with ice cream and simply held it there, your sense organs would adapt to its presence, and it would lose its taste: the sensation/perception link of impermanence.

When we think about how our "sense doors," including our mental sense door, can lead to attachment (and its negative, aversion), many other common examples come to mind. Can you eat just one peanut? Can the mere thought of your beloved trigger obsessional desire? Can the thought of someone who has treated you unjustly cause anger? Did you decide when you were young which political party you wanted to join? So often, mental formations are the skandha that causes attachment— to people, to objects, to ideas—and therefore suffering.

Early Ch'an masters such as the Fourth Ancestor, Tao-hsin, and his successor, Hung-jen, urged novices to spend a great deal of time contemplating the skandhas, which are like "layered clouds" shutting out the light of our true nature. When we follow this advice, we become conscious of the impermanent nature of the skandhas and thus of ourselves. Zen teacher Jisho Warner puts it this way: "Impermanence is a great river of phenomena, of beings, things, and events, coming to be and passing away in dependence on each other. This natural order of things includes us, and its laws are our laws. We are an endless moving stream in an endless moving stream."

In fact, we begin to realize that the idea of oneself is just another concept, and the notions of a permanent, unchanging self that bind us begin to loosen. That slackening gives us great comfort and opens us to having a new kind of experience, which contemporary Vietnamese master Thich Nhat Hanh calls interbeing. The next line of Dogen's verse describes this experience.

"To forget the self is to be enlightened by the ten thousand things" is an essential teaching of Zen. Once we forget that

Buddha in teaching mudra.
In the teaching mudra,
the Buddha is enumerating
the Four Noble Truths.

small self, once we become open to ourselves as part of the universe, then everything enlightens us, everything teaches us.

A fundamental understanding in Zen Buddhism is that during this process, the *experience* rather than the description of the experience is the important element. Bodhidharma, the First Zen Ancestor, made the point that in Zen there is no reliance on words, letters, or anything other than personal, mystical experience and a transmission mind to mind, between one individual and another. That's why in Zen there's so much focus on having a teacher—and not just a teacher in the abstract. You can't just read someone's writings and really understand Zen. You need a teacher who actually works with you, probes you, asks you questions, and gives back answers. Zen study must be one to one, which is why there are not gigantic Zen communities and why there are many teachers at large centers.

To fully appreciate how we get from stepping into ourselves to being enlightened by the ten thousand things, it's helpful to look at the teachings from which Zen practice arose.

THE FOUR NOBLE TRUTHS

....

The Buddha's enlightenment under the bodhi tree was the culmination of years of searching for answers to fundamental
questions of our existence: Why do we live and die? What is the
nature of our existence? And in particular, why do we suffer?
After he saw into the nature of the self, he taught the Four
Noble Truths for forty-five years, beginning in the Deer Park,
near Sarnath, with the ascetics with whom he had traveled for
years. The Buddha was sometimes called the Great Physician,
and the Four Noble Truths are the diagnosis of the central
problem of our existence, what caused the problem, that there
is a solution for it, and what that "cure" is.

THE FIRST NOBLE TRUTH

The First Noble Truth is that *dukkha* is the intrinsic nature of existence. Although the Pali word *dukkha* is most often translated
as "suffering," that definition is incomplete and unsatisfactory—
though for simplicity we will often use it here. Dukkha is the
quality of dissatisfaction, discomfort, and impatience that is part
of our everyday life. Think of dukkha as an imperfect space at
the center of a wheel where the axle goes. Imagine that you
have a supermarket cart with such a faulty wheel, and the whole
time you're in the store, it goes *ka-thunk, ka-thunk, ka-thunk* as
you go through the aisles. That's the quality of this "suffering."
For some of us, it's horrible suffering—physical pain, death of
or separation from loved ones, loss of money or prestige. For
others, just as deeply do they feel a kind of ambiguous dissatisfaction—what the existentialists call angst, or ennui.

In our culture, when we feel this discomfort, we take an

aspirin, have a drink, watch some television—do something else. We are unable to open ourselves and contain that feeling of discomfort and dissatisfaction. But the Buddha's teaching is that dukkha is inherent in human existence. An aspect of what it means to be alive is to feel this way. If we understand and appreciate this reality, then we have a different relationship to our feelings of imbalance and dissatisfaction as we approach the other three Noble Truths.

When they are first introduced to the First Noble Truth, many people become depressed—as if this were a tragic truth. But if you think of famous Buddhists of our century—the laughter of the Dalai Lama or the smile of Thich Nhat Hanh— it's clear that they are not manifesting gloom and doom. They're embodying something else: a kind of joy and openness that comes out of understanding the First Noble Truth, of understanding that suffering and joy are not two separate things.

THE SECOND NOBLE TRUTH

After the diagnosis of the problem, which is that we all experience dukkha, the Second Noble Truth is that suffering is caused by our desire for things to be different from the way they are. No matter what the situation, even something physical like a backache, beyond the physical pain most of the *suffering* comes from not wanting the situation to be this way—pulling away from the backache, not being present to it, not accepting it.

We have this experience also when we can't sleep at night. Most people become anxious or fret when they can't sleep, which wakes them up even more. When you stop fighting being awake, you've got a better chance of falling asleep. Besides, although it's more refreshing if you do sleep, you can rest your body and your mind even if you don't sleep. As the old saying goes, "Nobody ever died from lack of sleep."

If you think about every situation in which you've felt discomfort in the last several hours—whether physically or at work or with your partner—you'll find that you wanted something to be different. So you're grasping after what? You're grasping after an idea you have about the way reality *should* be, rather than simply being present for what *is*. Being present for what is does not mean that you don't work to create social change and to better yourself—it is not passive acceptance. But it is being aware of what really is in this moment.

The Buddha taught that this is a vicious circle where a certain amount of suffering arises, we want things to be different, so we create even more suffering. It's a lesson that we seem to have to learn over and over again. The pattern is especially evident in people with great physical suffering—for example, people who are quite ill with AIDS or suffering from drug reactions or other physical problems. When they're able to let go of the fear and anger around their condition—that thing we call dukkha—and can simply be present to the physical sensations that they're having, the overwhelming level of suffering decreases. You can see it for yourself the next time you have a cramp in your foot. Rather than tightening to the cramp, let go completely as if you're sending your mind right into your foot—and just be present to the cramp. See what happens. It's amazing how it just dissolves.

THE THIRD NOBLE TRUTH

The Third Noble Truth is that there is an end to the cycle of wanting something, having dissatisfaction, wanting things to be different, and constantly creating suffering within yourself. The Third Noble Truth affirms the existence of *nirvana*—which literally means "blown out"—a situation where that cycle does not exist.

The existence of nirvana as something or somewhere you can find is a point where Zen differs from other traditions. *Samsara* is our day-to-day life, the phenomenal world—it's not separate from the capability of being free from suffering. Zen Buddhism says that when we're awake and aware in our daily life and have broken the cycle of wanting things to be different, this is nirvana. Samsara is nirvana. The Third Noble Truth, then, tells us that there is a way out of dukkha within our own lives.

THE FOURTH NOBLE TRUTH:
THE EIGHTFOLD PATH

The Fourth Noble Truth shows how in samsara—in daily life— the Eightfold Path can lead to nirvana, to the relinquishing of grasping and suffering. In Zen Buddhism, the Eightfold Path is usually considered along with the sixteen Bodhisattva Precepts, which we will take up in detail next. But it's useful to look briefly at the Eightfold Path first.

The Eightfold Path begins with things that you do with your body and your mouth: Right Action, Right Speech, and Right Livelihood. *Right Action* is trying to do the right thing. *Right Speech* is trying to say the right thing, and clearly what you say affects your own psyche and others' as much as what you do. *Right Livelihood*—earning your living in the right way—is missing from many religious traditions, but it is basic to how you live your life.

The next two—Right Thought and Right View—are things

that you do with your mind. How you manage your thoughts is important to whether you're getting on the wheel of suffering and grasping or getting off and finding nirvana. *Right Thought* is interesting because, from the Zen Buddhist perspective, what you think is just as important as what you do. In the opening verse of the *Dhammapada*, a collection of the Buddha's sayings, he states, "All that we are is a result of what we have thought." Even if you're silently hating someone across the room, you're creating something: Aversion or desire is arising. *Right View*, on the other hand, has to do with your understanding of the world so that you can experience your life with wisdom and compassion, rather than with discouragement and aversion.

The last three—Right Mindfulness, Right Concentration, and Right Effort—refer to aspects of meditation, aspects of discipline for the mind. *Right Mindfulness* is awareness during everything you do in your life; it's important because awareness is what's going to get you off that wheel. Robert Aitken, in *The Gateless Barrier*, described how even a simple, familiar sound can derail mindfulness:

> Senzaki Sensei used to ask, "When you hear a dog bark, do you think of your own dog?" That is a very interesting question. For if you do, then very soon—immediately, in fact—you are running through the fields in a totally different place and time. You are following up on the sound and its associations— on and on. Your mind is unsettled, and so you are led around by sounds and forms. You are at the mercy of the bark. When you are at rest in silence, however, that bark is at your mercy—your own bark.

Right Concentration, or meditation, is taking the time to "step into yourself" and really be aware of the workings of your mind and body—to allow yourself to let go and just be in great emptiness. Right Concentration is an extraordinary tonic and comfort that allows you moments as if you're in nirvana. *Right Effort* is critical, because *none of this is easy at all.* But to have that good effort in mindfulness meditation—to just go ahead and do it, over and over and over again—is very empowering and transformative and helps us to bring that effort to everything else that we do.

There are many opportunities to practice Right Effort. As an exercise, pick a daily activity such as brushing your teeth, taking a shower, or making a bed. It can't be something that takes too long, or you won't be able to do the exercise, which is simply to be aware of every moment. If you can be completely mindful for that period of time, it's as powerful as a meditation on your cushion. Recognizing what we do with our minds, how unpresent we often are, and how delicious whatever we're doing *can* be—these insights can make even the most mundane activities delightful and nourishing.

Each of the three major traditions embraces the Four Noble Truths but emphasizes a different aspect of the Eightfold Path in general practice. Vipassana/Theravada says that you must have morality (*sila*—Right Speech, Action, and Livelihood) to be able to meditate and have right understanding. The Tibetans, on the other hand, believe that sila must be the foundation but stress Right Thought and Right View: Understand, study, debate, learn, practice your thought, and you will have good morality and good meditation. Zen emphasizes meditation, *samadhi*: Have Right Mindfulness, Concentration, and Effort, and you cannot help but observe sila and have right understanding. None of these traditions says, "Only my way," and all practice all parts of the Eightfold Path. But each stresses a different area, and for Zen it is meditation, the calm-ing of the mind.

Zen master Dogen, in *Moon in a Dewdrop*, told us in a straightforward way how to achieve the goal of the Eightfold Path:

> There is a simple way to become a buddha: When you refrain from unwholesome action, are not attached to birth and death, and are compassionate toward all sentient beings, respectful to seniors and kind to juniors, not excluding or desiring anything, with no designing thoughts or worries, you will be called a buddha. Do not seek anything else.

Again, simple but not easy.

THE BODHISATTVA PRECEPTS

In Zen Buddhism, the overarching emphasis is on meditation, but someone who decides to become a Zen Buddhist eventu-ally—perhaps after several years—will be introduced to the six-teen Bodhisattva Precepts, will study them for a period of time, then will decide whether to commit to living by them in a for-mal ceremony. We're acting within the sphere of these precepts all the time, but it can take many years of practice to fully appreciate their subtleties. Some very early teachers in fact saw little reason to instruct their students in the precepts because they felt that only a fully enlightened being could distinguish good from evil and know how to live accordingly. As our prac-tice deepens, we become increasingly mindful of our actions and their effects on others, and the goal of practice subtly shifts to being for the benefit of others. Formally, our commitment through these precepts is to become a *bodhisattva,* a being who seeks enlightenment in order to end the suffering and bring about the enlightenment of all other beings. But it is important always to be gentle with ourselves and not use "failures" to follow the precepts "perfectly" as battering rams against ourselves.

Often the word *vow* is used within the context of the Bodhisattva Precepts and the Four Vows (page 136), and the word can disconcert us if we think of it in the usual sense of a promise to someone or something else. In Zen Buddhism, a vow is an intention that, because of our nonseparation from others, we make to ourselves. When we can't keep our vow perfectly, we "repent" by doing zazen and contemplating the true nature of all things. In formal settings such as sesshins, we renew our vows three or more times daily, as reminders and as acknowledgment that we keep them imperfectly.

THE THREE TREASURES

The first three precepts are called the Three Treasures:

> Be one with the Buddha.
> Be one with the Dharma.
> Be one with the Sangha.

By taking refuge in the Three Treasures, we acknowledge our oneness with every aspect of the practice. The realization of oneness is an aspect of enlightenment that may be difficult for you to grasp in the beginning of your practice. Although you may not experience this equality with and nondifferentiation from all other beings fully and immediately, over time you will know it with increasing depth.

In the first Treasure, we become one with our own Buddha-nature. We realize that the Buddha is not a figure on the altar—that we are the Buddha, that we are one with (we have) the potential for awakening that is Buddhahood. In this way, the first Treasure is the truth of our nature and its potential.

The second Treasure is becoming one with the teachings, the Dharma. The teachings are boundless, not just old sutras or stories people have handed down. The teachings are subways and bread and cactuses—everything in the world, each of the "ten thousand things," is a teaching and is constantly expounding the Dharma. In this Treasure, we become one with all the things that are. So first we became one with one (the Buddhahood within us), then we become one without differentiation with everything there is: the teachings, the Dharma.

Third, we become one with the sangha, the community of practitioners. On a small scale, the sangha is the people we sit with where we sit, but on a large scale, the Sangha is every being in the universe.

While giving the Wisdom Teachings in New York in 1998, the Dalai Lama succinctly expressed the Mahayana teachings on the Three Treasures when he said that the first Treasure is recognizing our own Buddha-nature; the second Treasure, the Dharma, is the ultimate Wisdom that all things are empty of a permanent, separate self-nature; and that this wisdom enables us to be one with the third Treasure, the Sangha of all beings, thus realizing our Buddha-nature and acknowledging the first Treasure.

The next three are the *Three Pure Precepts*:

Not doing evil.

Doing good.

Doing good for others.

The Three Pure Precepts are very deceptive because they sound so similar, but each one reveals different aspects of our lives as bodhisattvas.

Not doing evil is the precept of not creating any evil. And how do you create evil? Ironically, you create evil by making any distinction between evil and good, by coming from any place of knowing. Zen master Bernie Glassman calls this precept "giving up fixed ideas about myself and the universe."

The second Pure Precept is *doing good*. This precept allows that there nevertheless exist differences, and when we see the differences, we bear witness. Some people believe that being an informed voter in a democratic election is a way of applying this precept. Bearing witness involves not just opening ourselves to positive experiences but also to negative, painful experiences such as the dying of a loved one or the hunger of a homeless panhandler. One recent example of bearing witness to atrocities is the annual retreats that the Zen Peacemaker Order has held at concentration camps where millions of Jews died during World War II. The experience of bearing witness was beautifully expressed by teacher Nancy Mujo Baker:

> I was just looking at the last line of the meal gatha—"May we exist in muddy water with purity like a lotus." I remember one day reciting this with everyone when it suddenly

dawned on me that being one with the muddy water is the purity of the lotus. I think we could say that bearing witness to the muddy water is the purity of the lotus.

The third Pure Precept is *doing good for others,* which is similar to the second Pure Precept but is much more active. It's wiping the wounds of the person who is suffering. It's all the social actions Zen Buddhists take to help others, whether a single act such as assisting someone to cross a street or a long-term commitment such as choosing to enter a helping profession, founding a hospice, or being of service as a volunteer.

You may face a situation where you eventually experience all three reactions: First, don't create evil—just be there. Second, witness. Third, act. All three may come quite quickly as, for example, when you encounter a homeless panhandler on the street: First, you see the panhandler but make no judgments

about why someone is homeless or panhandling or whether they want money for alcohol or drugs. Second, rather than making the panhandler "invisible" by looking away from him or her, you make eye contact and see the panhandler as someone not really separate from yourself. Third, you say a few kind words and put some change into the panhandler's stained coffee cup.

Buddha in Fear Not mudra.
In this gesture of comfort, the Buddha communicates, "Fear Not."

The Three Pure Precepts become the foundation for the next ten, the *Grave,* or Cardinal, *Precepts*: not killing; not stealing; not misusing sex; not telling lies; not using intoxicants; not talking about others' errors and faults; not elevating oneself and blaming others; not being stingy; not being angry; and not speaking ill of the Three Treasures. All these precepts can be taken from different points of view—and are, in different traditions. For example, regarding *not stealing,* the Vipassana / Theravada teaching is very specific: Never take something that has not been offered. But the Mahayana perspective would be: In some cases, you have to take something in order to give it to someone else. If there is a case where you must steal, you could also take the outlook position that everything belongs to everyone—there's nothing to be stolen—there's just oneness. You can take that prism and examine each precept from those three points of view to show that the precepts are not rules to be submitted to—but rather are a living phenomenon that, when followed with reverence and understanding, is the Noble Eightfold Path. In one form of practice, the precepts are used, one at a time, as koans. Similarly, if you want to truly experience the precepts, sit with one precept each week and really examine it. Let's look briefly at each one.

1. Not Killing

Clearly to live is to kill. With each breath we take, minuscule microbes are being breathed in. When we eat, we kill. What is nonkilling? In the end, it's a reverence for life. But what if you're a cook, for example, getting rid of roaches and rats in the kitchen to maintain the health of those who will eat the food you prepare? Such decisions are not always clear-cut. You have to be present to the context and the experience of the situation. Sometimes there are alternatives—for example, putting a screen in a window rather than using a flyswatter. For many, this precept means not to take life unnecessarily.

2. Not Stealing

In contemporary society, this precept isn't just about grabbing an apple from an applecart. You have to look at the items you buy and the investments you make, for this precept is about having things and not having things and deeply involves the environment and all our resources. To spend a week thinking about all the instances of not taking things but rather of supporting the nourishment of life on this planet is a powerful experience. You find yourself questioning how long your showers are, how far you go to recycle even when it's inconvenient, what kind of mileage you'd get on the designer sports utility vehicle you want, even where you shop and eat.

3. Not Misusing Sex

This precept is really about respect for another. Not misusing sex has nothing to do with whether a person is gay or lesbian or heterosexual or with the various sexual situations that might occur. It has to do with whether you are honoring the other person and yourself. Some people feel that not treating yourself or another person as an object is a suitable guideline for this precept. Others are more proscriptive and say that you should not engage in sex with a person if either of you is in a committed relationship.

4. Not Telling Lies

Telling lies arises from an inability or unwillingness to see the situation as it is, to speak and listen genuinely from the heart. To actively practice not lying to yourself is liberating. To not lie to others liberates them as well.

5. Not Using Intoxicants

This precept is about not being intoxicated with chemical substances, with ideas, with anything. It doesn't mean that a person can't have a glass of wine with dinner. The precept is not to cloud the mind, which is basically pure and undefiled.

6. Not Talking About Others' Errors and Faults

On the first level, we need to be able to notice when we're running others down, because that same critic is running us down, is running down the Buddha, is running down all of life and all that is nurturing and wonderful. This chain reaction creates very negative energy. On the other hand, this precept does not mean that we shouldn't talk about social problems, political issues, even difficulties in our sangha. It doesn't mean being passive. From the Mahayana perspective, for example, you *should* talk about governmental errors as loudly as you can. When you do so with a "little mind," then people just think you're another crank. But with the compassionate mind and the heart of the Mahayana, you'll be effective. Thich Nhat Hanh's recommendation for interacting with elected officials is not to rant and rave at them but rather to send them "love letters" laying out your position.

7. Not Elevating Oneself and Blaming Others

We've all experienced the desire to make ourselves look good or to point the finger at someone else as the cause of a difficulty. The link between *not elevating ourselves* and *blaming others* is sometimes hard to see, but they are two aspects of the same phenomenon: Both cause us to separate ourselves from others. Remember, these precepts are about the Eightfold Path, which is intended to save us from doing something that will create pain and suffering in our lives—as separation from others always does.

8. Not Being Stingy

Not holding back and always being willing to give have to do with the Dharma, as well as with the giving of material things. This precept includes always being able to express the Dharma when it's appropriate—not with dead words, but with actions in your life.

9. Not Being Angry

This is an important precept for Americans because we are told that we need to express our anger, but we're also told not to express our anger as we grow up. It's a confusing and difficult precept for many people—perhaps the most confusing. It's important to acknowledge feelings of anger and to be really present to them. The aim is not to eliminate anger when it arises but rather to accommodate it, to create a space for it. In a very paradoxical Zen way, we say, "Not being angry is being angry." *Not being angry* is to allow what is occurring to be there but not to hold on to it or fan it. If you push anger down and deny it, it seethes underneath. Awareness of your state of mind, of anger, is important. *Not being angry* is being aware of what you're feeling—and thus transforming the anger into wisdom.

10. Not Speaking Ill of the Three Treasures

Doubt is an important part of every practice. "Good doubt" is like salt—you need it. It's fine to challenge and to ask questions, but to speak ill of the Three Treasures weakens *your* faith and the faith of those around you.

SIXTEEN OBSERVANCES

OF THE ZEN PEACEMAKER ORDER

Whenever we look at precepts and vows, the first question is often "How do I do that?" Sometimes getting someone else's perspective can help answer that question. Within Zen Buddhism, the Zen Peacemaker Order, founded to link people who are engaged in social action and Zen Buddhism (see chapter 9), has given serious consideration to how their commitment to engaged Buddhism is expressed through the sixteen Bodhisattva Precepts. Here is how they first drafted their observance of these precepts.

Three Refuges of a Zen Peacemaker

Inviting all creations into the mandala of my practice and vowing to serve them, I take refuge in:

> **Buddha**, the awakened nature of all beings
> **Dharma**, the ocean of wisdom and compassion
> **Sangha**, the community of those living in harmony with all Buddhas and Dharmas

Three Tenets of a Zen Peacemaker

Taking refuge and entering the stream of Engaged Spirituality, I vow to live the life of:

Not-knowing, thereby giving up fixed ideas about myself
and the universe
Bearing witness to the joy and suffering of the world
Healing myself and others

Ten Practices of a Zen Peacemaker

Being Mindful of the interdependence of Oneness and
Diversity, and wishing to actualize my vows, I engage in the
spiritual practices of:

1. Recognizing that I am not separate from all that is. This is
   the precept of Non-Killing.
2. Being satisfied with what I have. This is the precept of Non-
   Stealing.
3. Encountering all creations with respect and dignity. This is
   the precept of Chaste Conduct.
4. Listening and speaking from the heart. This is the precept
   of Non-Lying.
5. Cultivating a mind that sees clearly. This is the precept of
   Not Being Deluded.
6. Unconditionally accepting what each moment has to offer.
   This is the precept of Not Talking About Others' Errors
   and Faults.
7. Speaking what I perceive to be the truth without guilt or
   blame. This is the precept of Not Elevating Oneself and
   Blaming Others.
8. Using all of the ingredients of my life. This is the precept
   of Not Being Stingy.
9. Transforming suffering into wisdom. This is the precept of
   Not Being Angry.
10. Honoring my life as an instrument of peacemaking. This is
    the precept of Not Thinking Ill of the Three Treasures.

Study of the precepts is usually begun after a long period of practice because in the beginning it's too easy to misinterpret them and to rationalize with the prism of multiple perspectives. Many people tend to judge themselves harshly when they begin to work with the precepts, because they can't see how they can ever match up to the precepts. And if they're judging themselves harshly, they're also judging the rest of the world that way. So what we end up with is an occasion for suffering.

Teachers deal with the precepts in an ongoing way as an integral—even if not explicitly stated—part of the way we live our lives. The sixteen precepts were originally built around preserving a community and its practice. Each precept is important to keeping alive the bodhisattva spirit and way of life. Strict and total observance of the precepts is an impossible task. But how admirable of us to try to observe them for reasons of karma.

KARMA

The word *karma* has become part of American jargon—you hear it in sentences like "That happened because you've got good karma." There are even signs in coffeehouses that say, "Tipping Is Karma Boomerang."

But in Buddhism, this term has a specific meaning that underlies many basic teachings. Understood in a very ordinary way, *karma* means "action" or "deed," though *karma* also refers to the fruit of action, to what comes out of action—karma is cause and effect. The Sanskrit word means "the manifestation of creation"—in other words, *karma* means that we are what we do. If you understand that you are part of everything in the universe, then you begin to understand that what you say and what you do affect everything in the universe. We know from ecological studies that a forest fire in Brazil will have an effect in North America. It's a little harder to see how the small things we do—the blink of an eye—have effects. But if you can appreciate the whole universe as a living entity, then anything that happens within that universe is going to affect everything else in that universe. That's karma.

A concept that is related to karma is *conditional arising,* or *dependent origination. This* arises, and therefore *that* arises. Everything is interconnected and interdependent, and anything arising within the grid is going to affect everything else on the grid. It's not always easy to see a direct cause and effect, but you can see it in a broader sense that when one thing happens, then another thing happens.

Zen Buddhism does not consider the intentionality of actions producing karma. Karma is neither good nor bad. It's just the reaction. Several years ago, a woman's accelerator jammed, and her car ran into a park and hit a number of people. She had no intentionality, but she killed and injured many people. That's karma. There was an action, and the reaction was that people were killed. When we bring intentionality into it, we're putting the light back on the individual, but karma is really the workings of the universe.

If you talk about karma in terms of the Eightfold Path, the first grouping is Right Speech, Action, and Livelihood, so it's easy to understand karma as action, as what happens. But when you consider Right Thought, karma is very subtle because it's internal: Karma starts with the thought pattern and has an effect right inside your mind. If you say something, it clearly affects the people around you. Any thought that you have is going to affect *you*, so the karma is internal but it will eventually affect others around you because it has affected you. Thus, a Zen student is living some of her teacher's karma—and so too all the way back to Bodhidharma and the Buddha. But also Hitler's and Caruso's. Their karma is what we're living out. So what's karma? It's not just what you hold in your personal life. It's what has happened in the world. That means that you can think of your personal life as the world, and you can begin to see that you are interconnected with a universe in which nonduality is reality.

NONDUALITY

The word *nonduality* refers to having no separate self, to not seeing other people and things as different from yourself. There are two ways to appreciate the nondual: One way is to appreciate that within you is everything in the universe. At this moment, the whole universe exists within you—you can imagine that you have people from China and Peru and trees and microbes flowing through your veins. Another way is to see yourself as part of everything in the universe. This relationship is well expressed in the story, especially popular among Buddhists, of the ancient god Indra's creating a vast network of jewels, each of which reflects every other jewel and is reflected in every other jewel. You are one connection on Indra's Net—and anything that happens in that net is going to affect everything else in that net.

There's a Zen saying that the most intimate relationship you can have with anything is *not knowing*. This means that you have dropped away the separation between the knower and the known. There is nothing to know because you are it. There's extraordinary intimacy when we understand that we are part of the world in this way.

The concept of nonduality goes with the concept of emptiness, and they are brought together in a well-known koan. In Bodhidharma's famous interview with Emperor Wu, Wu asked Bodhidharma what merit had been obtained by all Wu's good works of building stupas and places of practice. Bodhidharma replied, "No merit whatsoever. All empty." He was referring to the concept that nothing has any permanent worth—that everything is empty and without definition. The emperor didn't understand at all. So he said, "Who is it that stands before me?" and Bodhidharma said, "I don't know." This koan alludes to emptiness and to the intimacy of not knowing, of nonseparation. Let's look a little more closely at the questions of emptiness and the mind of emptiness, which is Buddha-mind.

EMPTINESS

There's a story about the linguist Benjamin Lee Whorf that helps us to appreciate the way Zen Buddhism uses the word *emptiness*. Though best known as a scholar, Whorf trained as a chemical engineer and worked for some years as an insurance adjuster. He became interested in words when he was working on insurance claims involving gasoline tanks that blew up at a particular refinery. As he went around the plant, he discovered that there were NO SMOKING signs surrounding tanks that were full of gasoline, and there were no cigarette butts at all. But in the area where the tanks had signs saying EMPTY

TANKS—despite NO SMOKING signs—cigarette butts were everywhere. Now an empty gasoline tank is just as dangerous as a full tank, because it is *filled with fumes*. There were explosions because people refused to see that although the tank was empty, it was also full—of fumes.

One Japanese word for emptiness is *ku*, which means "sky" or "void"—so skylike or empty mind is ku. The idea is that ku is as empty as the sky—or you could say as full as the sky. So much depends on perceptions. One story that has come down to us tells how the Tibetan Buddhist teacher Chögyam Trungpa once stood in front of a room full of students. He held up a large white sheet of paper on which he had drawn a sort of floppy-looking V shape. He asked the students what he was holding a picture of. Everyone in the class agreed that it was a bird flying—some even embellished this by saying that it was a gull flying over the ocean. Finally, Chögyam Trungpa said, "No. It is not a picture of a bird flying across the sky. It is a picture of the sky, with a bird flying across."

The term *shunyata* is used for "emptiness" in the central teaching that everything is impermanent and lacks a self-nature. (The relationship between form and emptiness is the theme of *The Heart Sutra*, presented in chapter 7.) Emptiness means that if you strip away all definitions and notions of each and every thing and just allow it to be, you see its interconnectedness with all other things. When we say that I am empty, what am I empty of? All definitions of myself. I'm just here. Emptiness means being totally interconnected with all things and not limited or defined by words or ideas. There is nothing fixed about it. There's just a wonderful fullness, like the sky. Like the Buddha-mind.

BUDDHA-MIND

Buddha-mind, or Buddha-nature, is the mind of not-knowing. It is the mind of oneness—of complete intimacy with or awareness of the cosmic interrelatedness of all things, the interpenetration of all things. When we perceive things from the point of view of Buddha-mind, the mind sees all things as one. We can experience this oneness, but we can't understand it, because understanding presupposes separation.

So there are many stories in Zen about a monk who asks a teacher, "What is Buddha?" In one, the teacher will say, "Mind is Buddha." Later, when another monk comes to the same teacher and says, "What is Buddha?" the teacher will say, "No mind, no Buddha." Mind is not Buddha. Over and over again, the teachings of Zen are that you can't understand the oneness. As Zen master Dogen put it in *Moon in a Dewdrop*:

Mind itself is buddha.
Practice is difficult. Explanation is not difficult.
Not-mind. Not-buddha.
Explanation is difficult. Practice is not difficult.

The interconnection of all things is beautifully described in *The Avatamsaka Sutra* by the image of Indra's Net (page 124). But there's no such thing as Indra's Net. There's just you and me. But there's also no you and me. All of these ways of talking about the self, nonduality, emptiness—even impermanence—are concepts evolved through the years to describe the indescribable. On the one hand, there are proselike, academic models of understanding something that cannot be understood. On the other, Zen koans have evolved as a way to sidestep this method of appreciating things and to help people understand a mystical experience that is enlightenment—which is Buddha-mind.

ENLIGHTENMENT

Enlightenment is perceiving our place in the universe—recognizing our true self, who we really are. As Dogen noted, "If you want to attain such a thing, you must be such a person. Since you are such a person, why trouble about such a thing?" It's the awareness of ourselves as the world—as everything—based on our experience, rather than our knowledge, of the emptiness of the universe. Dogen also said, "People's attaining enlightenment is like the moon reflected in water. The moon does not get wet, the water isn't broken. Though it is a vast expansive light, it rests in a little bit of water—even the whole moon, the whole sky, rests in a dewdrop on the grass."

There are some wonderful stories about how we all have Buddha-nature but aren't aware of it. One amusing and instructive parable is the story of Enyadatta, told in *The Shurangama Sutra (Sutra of the Heroic One),* whose theme is enlightenment through zazen. Enyadatta was a very beautiful and very vain young woman who was preoccupied with her own image. One morning, she arose and grasped her mirror, as was her habit, to begin looking at her reflection, but when she looked into the mirror, she saw nothing. She was so traumatized that she ran around crying and yelling about her missing head and was so out of control that she was in danger of injuring herself. Her friends tried to tell her that she had a head, but she would not heed them. Finally, to protect her, they bound her to a pillar in her home—a situation often related to the quieting of the body in zazen—and continued to try to persuade her that she had a head. But she was unable to really see through her delusion until one of her friends picked up a piece of wood and whacked her on the head. When she shrieked in pain, she suddenly knew that she had a head—and had always had one.

Another parable about our hidden nature was told by sixth century Fourth Ch'an Ancestor Chih-i:

> Ordinary people caught in bondage are unaware and do not know, like blind children of a rich family sitting in a storehouse of treasures without seeing any of them, just bumping into them when they move and thus being wounded by the treasures.

Early in Zen's history, drawings began to be used to express the realization of enlightenment. In the twelfth century, Ch'an master Kuo-an is credited with formalizing earlier drawings into the ten pictures, commentaries, and verses known as the ten *Oxherding Pictures*: Seeking the Ox; Finding the Tracks; First Glimpse of the Ox; Catching the Ox (see page 130); Taming the Ox; Riding the Ox Home; Ox Forgotten, Self Alone; Both Ox and Self Forgotten; Returning to the Source; and Entering the Marketplace with Helping Hands. The *Oxherding Pictures* have continued to be an important focus of Zen study ever since, especially in Japan.

Two Japanese terms—*kensho* and *satori*—are often used interchangeably in Zen Buddhism for "enlightenment," though customarily, *satori* refers to the experience of the Buddha or Zen Ancestors and *kensho* to the individual's initial self-realization.

Once a person becomes enlightened, is he perfect? In a way. But in Zen, enlightenment is not a thing that happens in a flash

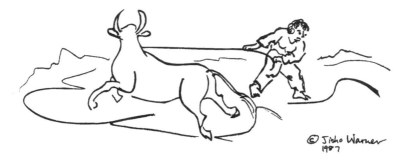

Oxherding Picture #4, *Catching the Ox.* *The unruly mind keeps dashing away, even as we struggle to catch and tame it. Perhaps trying to control it isn't the best way to harness its power after all. Zen practice aims for harmony between oxherder and ox, not opposition and strife.*

of white light and makes you permanently perfect. It's an *insight* that transforms the way you see all things in that moment. It's living a life that is permeated with the understanding that you're a part of all other things. As Muso Kokushi noted in the fourteenth century, "Those who have not yet attained enlightenment should study the intent rather than the expression, while those who have attained enlightenment should study the expression rather than the intent."

In Zen at a certain point a teacher may perceive and acknowledge the transformations that have occurred within a student over time. Customarily, when the teacher recognizes that the student surpasses the teacher, the teacher will transmit to the student mind to mind. And the student is "enlightened by the ten thousand things." But the verse at the beginning of this chapter did not end with these words. Dogen went on to tell us what happens next: "When actualized by the ten thousand things, your body and mind and the bodies and minds of others drop away."

Words of Wisdom and Joy

S E L E C T E D

T E X T S

SUTRAS (or *suttas* in Pali—literally "threads") are early teachings attributed to the Buddha, written down long after he spoke. As we noted in chapter 5, these teachings were transmitted only orally for several centuries. Some of the sutras used in the Mahayana tradition, such as *The Heart Sutra,* were discovered many years after the earliest teachings were recorded.

Thousands of pages of the sutras used in Zen Buddhism are now available in English translation. Some are studied and chanted, but others are usually only studied. Some are long and difficult; others are short and accessible. Here are examples of the kinds of sutras and chants used in services that you are most likely to encounter when you visit a zendo, as well as a description of the major sutras that are central to Zen teachings and that may be studied but not recited.

SUTRAS

The Heart Sutra and The Diamond Sutra—part of what is called the Wisdom (Prajna Paramita, or "wisdom that reaches the other shore") literature—teach that everything is empty: There is absolutely nothing to teach, nothing to gain—there's just *this*. These teachings were said to have been given by the Buddha to his students at Vulture Peak. The Heart Sutra is so frequently chanted in services and at sesshins that most students have memorized the version used in their temple. Because of the relationship between form and emptiness and the centralness of this teaching, probably more commentaries have been written on this sutra over the centuries than on any other.

THE HEART SUTRA
(Zen Center of Los Angeles)

Avalokiteshvara Bodhisattva, doing deep Prajna Paramita,
Clearly saw emptiness of all the five conditions.
Thus completely reliving misfortune and pain.

Oh Shariputra, form is no other than emptiness,
Emptiness no other than form.
Form is exactly emptiness, emptiness exactly form.
Sensation, conception, discrimination, awareness are likewise
    like this.

Oh Shariputra, all dharmas are forms of emptiness, not born,
Not destroyed, not stained, not pure, without loss, without gain.
So in emptiness there is no form, no sensation, conception,
    discrimination, awareness;

No eye, ear, nose, tongue, body, mind; no color, sound, smell,
taste, touch phenomena;
No realm of sight, no realm of consciousness, no ignorance and
no end to ignorance,
No old age and death and no end to old age and death,
No suffering, no cause of suffering, no extinguishing, no path, no
wisdom and no gain,
No gain and thus the Bodhisattva lives Prajna Paramita
With no hindrance in the mind, no hindrance therefore no fear.
Far beyond deluded thoughts this is Nirvana.
All past, present and future Buddhas live Prajna Paramita
And therefore attain Annutara Samyak Sambodhi.

Therefore know Prajna Paramita is the great mantra,
The vivid mantra, the best mantra, the unsurpassable mantra.
It completely clears all pain. This is the truth not a lie.
So set forth the Prajna Paramita Mantra, set forth this mantra
and say,
Gate Gate! Paragate! Parasamgate. Bodhi Svaha! Prajna
Heart Sutra.

OTHER SUTRAS

The Diamond Sutra

The Diamond Sutra, another part of the Wisdom teachings propounding emptiness, is the diamond-hard edge that cuts through delusion—especially the delusion that physical phenomena have reality beyond being projections of the mind—and leads to enlightenment, as its final words proclaim. So powerful is it that Hui-neng (Japanese, E'no, 638–713), the illiterate woodcutter who became the Sixth Ch'an Ancestor, was said to have had his first enlightenment experience when he heard *The Diamond Sutra* recited. He went north and became fully enlightened when the Fifth Ancestor recounted it to him and transmitted the mind seal that made Hui-neng his successor. Hui-neng was later believed to have composed the so-called *Platform Sutra*.

The Platform Sutra

The Platform Sutra, attributed to Hui-neng, tells much about the life of the Sixth Ancestor and expounds many of the teachings that would powerfully affect the shaping of Zen—especially the teaching that the Buddha-mind is within oneself and that it is there that the Buddha must be sought. Although scholars have proven that *The Platform Sutra* could not have been written at the time, according to the historical facts described in it, it has nevertheless been a rich source of teachings and debates, such as those over the gradual versus the sudden experience of enlightenment.

The Faith-Mind Sutra

The Faith-Mind Sutra is not really a sutra but is a seventh-century text attributed to the Third Ch'an Ancestor, Seng-t'san (Sosan in Japanese; died 606). Its teaching is to be present in this moment. If you simply avoid picking and choosing, you'll be aware of each moment just as it is. You will essentially experience nirvana. The most frequently cited verse is the opening:

The Great Way is not difficult at all;
Simply avoid picking and choosing.

The Vimalakirti Sutra

The Vimalakirti Sutra ("The Discourse of Vimalakirti," an early follower of the Buddha) is the teaching of not talking, of the thunderous silence that is the answer to any question because the teachings cannot really be talked about. A popular aspect of this sutra is that Vimalakirti, the wisest of the bodhisattvas, is a layperson.

The Lankavatara Sutra

The Lankavatara Sutra ("Sutra on the Descent to Sri Lanka") is a long sutra about how you simply have to experience the teachings, rather than writing or talking about them. As Dainin Katagiri noted in Returning to Silence, "The world of conceptualization is kind of a blueprint for a house. Through the blueprint you can imagine what the house will be like. Or you can build the house from the blueprint. So the blueprint is important. But a blueprint is a blueprint, and you cannot live there."

The Lotus Sutra

The Lotus Sutra is the "pearl" of literature and wisdom for all the Mahayana tradition, but especially the T'ien-t'ai (Japanese, Tendai) and Nichiren sects, which were founded on its teachings. The Lotus Sutra is said to have been given by the Buddha on Vulture Peak near the end of his life. It is beautifully written—the source of many of the metaphors, similes, and stories that you hear most often in Buddhism. One of the most popular, for example, tells the story of a man who went out drinking with his best friend until quite late one night. His friend, a very rich man, sewed a priceless jewel into the hem of his robe. But the man traveled over the world in poverty because he did not know he had it, just as we have a priceless jewel but are never aware of it. This central teaching of the possibility of enlightenment for all has contributed to *The Lotus Sutra*'s popularity.

THE FOUR VOWS

The Four Vows sound impossible, and that impossibility is their distinction. "Sentient Beings are numberless; I vow to save them." How do you do that? This is a koan. You begin with yourself. The paradoxical nature of the Four Vows is in your saying that you're going to do the impossible.

The traditional version of the Four Vows is used daily in services and individual practice. The Four Vows have also been adapted by Zen groups such as the socially engaged Zen Peacemaker Order and by individual sanghas.

THE FOUR VOWS
(Traditional translation)

Sentient Beings are numberless; I vow to save them.
Desires are inexhaustible; I vow to put an end to them.
The Dharmas are boundless; I vow to master them.
The Buddha Way is unsurpassable; I vow to attain it.

THE FOUR VOWS
(Zen Peacemaker Order version)

Creations are numberless; I vow to free them.
Delusions are inexhaustible; I vow to put an end to them.
Reality is boundless; I vow to perceive it.
The enlightened way is unsurpassable; I vow to embody it.

(Community of Mindfulness/New York Metro version,
inspired by the teachings of Thich Nhat Hanh)

This vows statement is scheduled after the Four Vows to address difficult situations of conflict that arise in our lives (or our sangha) when we are caught in the historical dimension. It is offered in this format as a means for deepening our willingness and capacity to meet these situations skillfully and to transform them in a wholesome way. The vows can be changed or spoken by an individual or together as a sangha. Language can be adapted as appropriate (*aspire to, determined to, undertake, committed to, greet,* for example). After using them, members of the sangha share their experiences with them.

1. Sangha well-being nourishes my well-being.
   My well-being nourishes sangha well-being.
      Anchored in conscious breathing,
      I vow to water the seeds of joy, understanding, and inclusiveness in myself and all beings.
2. Conflicts are inevitable.
      Anchored in conscious breathing,
      I vow to greet them with love and kindness.
3. Unwholesome mental formations—resentment, disappointment, fear, jealousy, anger, depression, despair, discouragement, doubt—are unavoidable.
      Anchored in conscious breathing,
      I vow to recognize and transform them.
4. Attachment and aversion are inescapable.
      Anchored in conscious breathing,
      I vow to see them, smile to them, and let them go.
5. Repeat 1 (Sangha well-being . . .).

GATHAS

....

Gathas ("verses" or "songs") are commonly chanted during rituals. The Morning Gatha affirms the way of liberation. By wearing the teachings of the *Tathagata* ("everythingness" or "suchness") in this moment, I save all sentient beings. We say the Evening Gatha every night to remind ourselves that for all the openness and beauty of the practice, there's also the need of immediacy to really practice. Other gathas are recited individually or as a group during other parts of services and zazen.

MORNING GATHA
(Verse of the Kesa, Zen Center of Los Angeles)

Vast is the robe of liberation,
A formless field of benefaction;
I wear the Tathagata teaching,
Saving all sentient beings.

Kesa verse. *On the back of the rakusu worn by the jukai initiate, her teacher has written the "Verse of the Kesa"— the verse of the similar patchwork bib worn by Zen masters.*

EVENING GATHA
(Zen Center of Los Angeles)

Let me respectfully remind you:
Life and death are of supreme importance;
Time passes swiftly by and opportunity is lost.
Each of us must strive to awaken.
Awaken! Take heed!
Do not squander your life!

GATHA OF ATONEMENT
(Zen Center of Los Angeles)

All evil karma ever committed by me since of old
On account of my beginningless greed, anger and ignorance;
Born of my body, speech and mind,
Now I atone for it all.

INCENSE OFFERING
(Plum Village Chanting and
Recitation Book)

In gratitude, we offer this incense of all Buddhas and
bodhisattvas throughout space and time.
May it be fragrant as Earth herself, reflecting our careful efforts,
our wholehearted awareness, and the fruit of understanding,
slowly ripening.
May we and all beings be companions of Buddhas and
bodhisattvas.
May we awaken from forgetfulness and realize our true home.

SUTRA OPENING GATHA
*(Plum Village Chanting and
Recitation Book)*

The Dharma is deep and lovely.
We now have a chance to see it,
study it, and practice it.
I vow to realize its true meaning.

SUTRA CLOSING GATHA
*(Plum Village Chanting and
Recitation Book)*

Reciting the sutras, practicing the way of awareness,
gives rise to benefits without limit.
I vow to share the fruits with all beings.
I vow to offer tribute to parents, teachers,
friends, and numerous beings
who give guidance and support along the path.

GATHA FOR ENTERING
THE MEDITATION HALL
*(Plum Village Chanting and
Recitation Book)*

Entering the meditation hall,
I see my true mind.
I vow that once I sit down,
all disturbances will stop.

GATHA FOR SITTING DOWN IN THE MEDITATION HALL

(Plum Village Chanting and Recitation Book)

Sitting here
is like sitting under the Bodhi tree.
My body is mindfulness itself,
entirely free of distractions.

8

Dispelling Delusions

FREQUENTLY

ASKED

QUESTIONS

People have walked right through this door, squinted at me, and asked me, "Are you enlightened?" I've squinted right back and replied, "Not at this moment."

PAT ENKYO O'HARA

WHAT IS ENLIGHTENMENT?
Enlightenment is to see into your true nature—to experience your oneness with all things. To be free of the delusion that you are a separate self. It is important not to reify enlightenment as a *thing* that you get, as if it were permanent and solid. It's an awareness.

WHAT IS NIRVANA?
The word *nirvana* means "blown out" or "no wind." Nirvana is

the state of being where there is no grasping, no desire for things to be different from the way they are. We seek nirvana in everyday life, in samsara—in those moments of life when we are able to not be grasping, when we're able to be present to the moment, to now, to our lives as they are, to understanding our relationship to the universe. In those moments, we are experiencing our life as nirvana.

WHY DO ORDAINED ZEN BUDDHISTS SHAVE THEIR HEADS?

The tradition goes all the way back to the time of the Buddha, when it was fashionable to have beautiful long hair, scented with perfume. The Buddha shaved his head and shaved the heads of his followers as a symbol of letting go of attachment, especially to physical beauty. Throughout the history of Buddhism, the practice was maintained as a traditional way of letting go of attachments and as a visible sign of the renunciant's life. American women Zen priests—many of whom play multiple roles in society—are no longer required to shave their heads. But many still do, as a way to remind themselves of their main practice of serving others.

WHAT DO THE DIFFERENT TITLES USED IN ZEN MEAN?

Many of the titles are specific to a Zen center and are not necessarily global in definition. The terms *monk* and *priest,* for example, are used interchangeably at some centers, but at others a monk is someone who has taken a vow of celibacy and lives in a monastery; a priest may not do so. Both titles imply that an ordination *(tokudo)* has taken place and that the person has made vows, wears priestly robes, and is trained to officiate at services and rituals. Typically, a Zen teacher is called by the title *sensei* ("teacher"), which implies that the teacher has received recognition from his or her teacher and can independently carry out all teaching activities. The title *roshi* ("old teacher") in some lineages is given as an ultimate empowerment, usually after many years of teaching, but in other traditions it is conferred simply when people begin to refer to their sensei as roshi. *Dharma holder* and *senior student* designate someone who is far along in their Zen studies and is often entrusted with teaching responsibilities, under the guidance of his or her sensei. *Dharma heir* is someone who has received direct transmission from their roshi.

IS THERE A CONFLICT BETWEEN ZEN PRACTICE AND BELIEF IN ANOTHER RELIGION?

No. Whether you are Catholic, Jewish, Muslim, or any other faith, there is no conflict from the Zen point of view. A person can be a Catholic priest, a rabbi, or a strong practitioner in any religion and also practice Zen. Zen, being nontheistic, simply doesn't address the question of whether there's a god or not, so the only discord that might arise would come from the other tradition.

ISN'T IT IDOLATRY TO BOW TO STATUES OF THE BUDDHA?

No, although the main objection to Buddhist practice that comes up for people of some faiths is bowing. You'll hear statements like "I'm not allowed to bow to idols, and I object to bowing to idols. That's bad." But Buddhists perceive the images on our altars as reminders of our own Buddha-consciousness, as well as the consciousness of all those who have become awakened or taught in the past. We don't see a difference between those people and ourselves. Because we believe that all things are one, we're not bowing to an idol—rather, we're bowing to the Buddha, to Buddha-nature, and to a continuation of the Buddha-mind throughout all states and time, as actualized by ourselves.

WHY WOULDN'T THE BUDDHA ANSWER CERTAIN QUESTIONS, SUCH AS THE EXISTENCE OF A CREATOR GOD?
Metaphysical questions are concepts that exist in the mind and can be a very useful way of understanding the universe. But the Buddha emphasized direct experience of what is in your life right now. To explain why he would not answer such questions, he told the story of a man who was shot with an arrow. Suppose, when the Buddha said, "I can take the arrow out," the man said, "No, I won't allow you to take the arrow out as I'm sitting here bleeding until you explain to me where the arrow came from, who shot it, and what it was made out of." The man would bleed to death seeking answers to questions that couldn't stanch his wound. The endless metaphysical questions are simply not a good use of the Buddha's time—then or now.

ARE ZEN BUDDHISTS ANTI-INTELLECTUAL?
No. That accusation sometimes arises because we try to break apart the very moment that one is conceptualizing. Quite the opposite is true: One of the challenges that Zen Buddhism in the West faces is *not* to be so intellectual—not to be attractive *only* to intellectuals. Zen is attractive but also is sometimes very frustrating to well-educated people who are used to figuring things out. When Zen asks them to use another part of their

mind, not the cognitive, that's when they complain that it's anti-intellectual.

WHAT IS "ZEN MIND"?

It's not the intellectual mind but that deeper cognition that understands or that experiences the whole world as itself and itself as the whole world. It's the mind of emptiness.

WHAT IS "BEGINNER'S MIND"?

It's the ability to encounter each experience with fresh innocence, as if for the first time.

WHAT'S THE MAIN DIFFERENCE BETWEEN THE SOTO AND RINZAI TRADITIONS?

Zazen is the heart of both traditions, and teachers in both—at least in this country—may use koans. But the emphases are different: Soto stresses meditation (shikantaza), while Rinzai stresses koans.

WHY DO SOME BUDDHISTS FACE THE WALL WHEN THEY MEDITATE?

It's a Soto Zen practice to face the wall during meditation. Some people relate the practice to a legend about the sixth-century Indian teacher Bodhidharma, the First Ch'an Ancestor of China, who is said to have settled at Shaolin monastery in northern India and sat facing the wall of a cave for nine years. Actually, Soto Zen practitioners face the wall for a very simple reason: It's less distracting. When you face outward and someone across the room scratches his nose, you see it and you say, "Now why is he doing that? He shouldn't be doing that. Doesn't he know . . . ?"

DO ZEN BUDDHISTS BELIEVE IN REINCARNATION?

Zen Buddhists don't use the term *reincarnation*. Zen Buddhists use the term *rebirth* but don't talk about rebirth in a physical way—where a person dies and comes back as a crocodile or another person on the other side of the planet. The word *rebirth* is used in a more metaphorical sense: When I die, I become one with all things. My rebirth is in all things. At the memorial service for someone who has died, the sentence "Nothing is taken away" is spoken. When a person is born, nothing is added. We're all one. Rebirth is simply another state of being.

ARE ZEN BUDDHISTS VEGETARIANS?

Not necessarily, although it depends on the country of origin. The Chinese Zen Buddhists are vegetarians, as are all Chinese Buddhists. Korean and Vietnamese Zen Buddhists are vegetarians. Japanese Zen Buddhists are not. And American Zen Buddhists tend to be all over the lot—from strict vegetarian to meat eaters.

HOW ARE ZEN TEACHERS AND CENTERS FINANCIALLY SUPPORTED?

Typically, a Zen center raises money by donations or dues from its sangha, by retreats and workshops, by general fundraising, and by Right Livelihood projects. Usually no one of these is enough to sustain a community. Retreats and workshops do not generate enough to cover all of a center's expenses but can help stabilize a community's budget. Sangha dues often pay for the salaries and expenses such as medical and Social Security payments of a teacher and staff. General fundraising is necessary for purchasing and maintaining the center's property and buildings. Many Zen communities pay small stipends to resident staff—be they teachers, monks, or laypeople. These stipends, medical insurance, housing, and food make up the "welfare" of the residents. The model generally followed is for funds to be given to the community, which then takes care of individuals. Some separate *dana* ("generosity") may be given to the teacher or to a "teacher's discretionary fund." As a rule, Zen teachers in this country are not wealthy, and some, with family responsibilities, may take on auxiliary work as writers, teachers, or therapists.

DOES ZEN BUDDHISM PUT ZAZEN ABOVE EVERY-THING ELSE?

It puts zazen in the *heart* of everything else. Zen literature is filled with warnings of the dangers of self-satisfied, passive meditation. Yet ultimately it is through zazen that we become capable of functioning with wisdom in the world. So yes, zazen is the heart of it.

9

Epilogue

ZEN IN

ACTION

*As you walk to the corner, you see a man huddled in a doorway. He is
sitting on a piece of cardboard, wrapped in a filthy coat. You can see
the bottle in a paper bag sticking out of his pocket. And you can hear
the plink of coins in the paper cup he shakes in your direction.
Looking down, you move to the outside of the sidewalk and think, "If
I give him change, he'll just spend it for booze." Then you catch yourself and wonder what happened to the spontaneous generosity that
was supposed to come with practice. And then you realize that at least
you caught yourself in these thoughts.*

MANY PEOPLE mistakenly assume that Buddhism is a world-
denying, inner-directed, isolating practice. But the Buddha's life
was a life of service, and his discourses frequently addressed
topics like generosity, peace, poverty, crime, and ecology. The
history of Buddhism is filled with examples of acting on these
concerns. Just because early Zen Buddhists lived in monasteries

Pat Enkyo O'Hara, Sensei, resident teacher of the Village Zendo in New York City, is active in the Zen Peacemaker Order, the AIDS Interfaith Network, and numerous national and local peacemaking projects. Here she addresses attendees at the annual Change Your Mind Day sponsored by Tricycle *magazine.*

didn't mean that they weren't involved in social action—that they were just up on a mountain. In fact, there's a long tradition of orphanages attached to Zen monasteries and of monks helping people. Social action—also known as *engaged Buddhism*—is a natural outcome of the practice and always has been.

Social action—in the broadest sense of taking care of everything that's in your life—comes out of and is inseparable from the inner changes that manifest in wisdom and compassion. Social action is sometimes global but is always personal. The personal—even intimate—nature of engaged Buddhism was well described by Lex Hixon in *Living Buddha Zen*:

> Without needing to generate any special motive of compassion, the left hand comes to the aid of the right hand when it runs into trouble. This dynamic oneness and mutuality of our

two hands, beyond meditation and premeditation, is the actual, moment-by-moment experience of emptiness as subjectless, objectless compassion. This perfect mutuality and inseparability of our two hands is beyond any verbal teaching, yet we all experience it clearly.

Thich Nhat Hanh, the Vietnamese Buddhist monk who was nominated by Martin Luther King, Jr., for the Nobel Peace Prize, is known for his worldwide efforts on behalf of peace, but his teachings always stress creating inner peace as the path to that larger goal. Some of his most moving statements deal with the individual within the family—describing how learning to be present through practice is the greatest gift of love we can offer. At the 1996 Peacemaking Conference in San Francisco, speaker after speaker emphasized that we must begin with ourselves before we can foster peace within our families, communities, and world.

In the United States, Zen practitioners have founded a number of organizations, such as the Buddhist Peace Fellowship, as a way of extending their practice and their sangha on behalf of resisting exploitation and violence and providing sanctuary for refugees and others in need. Zen Buddhists have been especially active, for example, in the hospice movement in the San Francisco Bay Area.

New vision has been given to engaged Buddhism by Bernie Glassman. Then abbot of the Zen Center of Los Angeles, he went to New York in 1979 to establish a Zen community. Glassman realized that there had to be a way for the community to support itself, while creating jobs and giving job training, so he started a catering business. People said, "That's not Zen. That's catering." But his followers learned to practice Zen while they were catering. Then he opened a bakery. People said, "That's not Zen. That's baking." Yes it is, so they learned to bake with their minds. Eventually, the community created a construction company to renovate abandoned apartment buildings as residences and offered them plus counseling and job training to formerly homeless people. Next he established another housing project for homeless people with AIDS. Glassman also began to hold retreats—not only in serene monastic settings but also on the sidewalks of New York City and at Auschwitz, the former Nazi concentration camp. He and his late wife also founded the Zen Peacemaker Order for people who are actively engaged in social action and are in some way associated with Zen Buddhism—for all of us who are awakened to our interconnectedness and are doing work wherever we may find it—whether in the environment or with hospice groups or with young children.

Each one of us will find our own way to live our lives mindfully with wisdom and compassion. Some of us will participate with others in social actions or will seek careers of service. But even at the individual level, we can bring our awareness to the world around us. Are we going against the spirit of the precepts in our relationship to resources? Do we recycle, take short showers, choose an automobile that gets high gasoline mileage, and buy products with responsible packaging? Do we invest in or financially support corporations that exploit their workers or pollute? Do we cheat on our taxes? Gossip? Do we take our one seat on our cushion regularly? Even our most mundane personal practices of transformation and interconnectedness can have an impact on the people and the world around us. Nothing is lost.

There's always been a base of social action associated with Zen, but now it's visible because so many lay practitioners in Zen have combined their practice with Right Livelihood as schoolteachers, psychotherapists, social workers, health care workers, and lawyers. Many others are volunteers in schools, prisons, shelters, and hospices. Many are environmental and human rights activists. Many of us have found that when we encounter a homeless man, we can meet his eyes and reach out to him.

10

SUGGESTIONS

FOR FURTHER

READING

BODHIDHARMA, the founder of Zen, is said to have stressed that we should not rely on words and letters. Ironically, when he brought Buddhism from India to China, Zen was adopted by the intelligentsia of China—all people skilled with letters and writing. So from its beginning, Zen has not been a completely oral tradition—koan study, for example, is based on written-down stories. But there always has been a tension in Zen between beautiful expression and a rejection of so-called dead words: words that tie us up with an idea—such as a fixed notion of what enlightenment is, what the Buddha way is, or what the benefits of meditation are. Every time we say *anything*, it's easy to set a trap for someone to get stuck in—even the idea of what Zen is. The trick is to write something that will encourage people to seek the truth without saying, "This is the Truth," and many of the sutras and books about Buddhism and Zen Buddhism do just that. The sutras and chants listed in chapter 7 are those most commonly used in Zen Buddhism, and the few books listed here were chosen because they are especially accessible to or important for new students of Zen or because they are closely related to a specific point or quotation in this book. In any case, read them with your beginner's mind.

BOOKS

Aitken, Robert. *Taking the Path of Zen*. San Francisco: North Point Press, 1982.
> An accessible guide to Zen Buddhism in a Western context, based on Aitken's orientation programs at Diamond Sangha training centers.

———. *The Gateless Barrier: The Wu-men Kuan (Mumonkan)*. San Francisco: North Point Press, 1991.
> A collection of the basic koans of Zen, gathered by Wu-men in the thirteenth century. The modern translation and commentary are by Roshi Robert Aitken.

Aoyama, Shundo. *Zen Seeds: Reflections of a Female Priest*. Tokyo: Kosei Publishing Co., 1990.
> A practical and illuminating collection of essays based on personal experience and extensive knowledge of sacred texts.

Beck, Charlotte Joko. *Everyday Zen*, edited by Steve Smith. San Francisco: HarperSanFrancisco, 1989.
> Zen integrated into Western lay life through this remarkable teacher's exploration of bringing practice to love and work.

Dogen, Zen Master. *Moon in a Dewdrop*. San Francisco: North Point Press, 1985.

Important essays by the thirteenth-century philosopher who brought Zen from China to Japan and founded Soto Zen Buddhism.

Glassman, Bernie. *Bearing Witness: A Zen Master's Lessons in Making Peace.* New York: Bell Tower, 1998.
The cofounder of the Zen Peacemaker Order demonstrates how each of the order's vows can be put into action to make peace.

———— and Rick Fields. *Instructions to the Cook: A Zen Master's Lessons in Living a Life That Matters.* New York: Bell Tower, 1996.
How to live a life of social responsibility, based on fundamental Zen teachings.

Hanh, Thich Nhat. *Being Peace.* Berkeley, CA: Parallax Press, 1987.
The importance of being peace in order to make peace.

————. *Old Path White Clouds.* Berkeley, CA: Parallax Press, 1991.
A beautifully told story of the Buddha's life and teachings, based on both Mahayana and Theravada texts.

————. *Zen Keys: A Guide to Zen Practice.* New York: Doubleday, 1974; rev. 1995.
Beginning with personal experiences, a clear presentation of basic Zen practices and beliefs.

Hixon, Lex. *Living Buddha Zen.* Burdett, NY: Larson Publications, 1995.
A re-creation of the spiritual transmissions from Shakyamuni Buddha's enlightenment through fifty-two generations of his successors.

Kapleau, Philip. *The Three Pillars of Zen.* 25th anniv. ed. New York: Anchor Books, 1989.
Truly an insider's guide to Zen, with detailed instructions and commentary on zazen and dokusan.

————. *Awakening to Zen.* New York: Scribner, 1997.
A collection of thirty years of teachings by a master of making Zen Buddhism accessible to Americans.

Katagiri, Dainin. *Returning to Silence: Zen Practice in Daily Life.* Boston: Shambhala, 1988.

A presentation of the basic teachings that emphasize that "Buddha is your daily life."

Kraft, Kenneth, ed. *Zen: Tradition and Transition.* New York: Grove Press, 1988.

A sourcebook of essays on Zen history and practice.

Mu Soeng. *Thousand Peaks: Korean Zen—Tradition and Teachers.* Cumberland, RI: Primary Point Press, 1991.

A comprehensive and accessible history of Korean Zen by a noted Buddhist scholar who is a former monk.

Reps, Paul. *Zen Flesh, Zen Bones: A Collection of Zen and Pre-Zen Writings.* Boston: Charles E. Tuttle, 1989.

A classic collection of Zen stories, now back in print in a handsome new edition.

Suzuki, Shunryu. *Zen Mind, Beginner's Mind.* New York: Weatherhill, 1970.

Teachings on Zen meditation and practice by one of the most influential Zen masters of his time.

Uchiyama, Kosho. *Opening the Hand of Thought: Approach to Zen.* New York: Viking Penguin, 1993.

Answers the question of how to bring Zen practice and our lives together into a fresh expression of our life-force.

11

ZEN CENTERS

AND RESOURCES

THROUGHOUT THE United States, the number of Zen Buddhist centers for study and meditation has been growing rapidly. Those listed below exist at the time of this writing and are included to help you find a center in your area. Many centers have newsletters that can give you information about events sponsored by the center, and major Buddhist magazines and the Internet carry listings.

ZEN CENTERS

NORTHEAST

Kinpuan—Zen Mountain
Monastery Affiliate
Albany, NY
518-432-4676

Living Dharma Center
P.O. Box 304
Amherst, MA 01004
413-259-1611

Barrington Zen Center
7 Lois Lane
Barrington, NH 03825
603-664-7654

Living Dharma Center
P.O. Box 513
Bolton, CT 06043
860-742-7049

Brooklyn Buddhist Association
211 Smith Street
Brooklyn, NY 11201
718-488-9511

Zen Center of New York City
Fire Lotus Temple
500 State Street
Brooklyn, NY 11217
718-875-8229

Zen Affiliate of Burlington
VT affiliate of Zen Mountain
Monastery (NY)
54 Rivermount Terrace
Burlington, VT 05401
802-658-6466

Cambridge Zen Center
199 Auburn Street
Cambridge, MA 02139
617-576-3229

Jizo-an Monastery
1603 Highland Avenue
Cinnaminson, NJ 08077
609-786-4150

The Kwan Um School of Zen
The Providence Zen Center
99 Pound Road
Cumberland, RI 02864
401-658-1476

Ch'an Meditation Center
90-56 Corona Avenue
Elmhurst, NY 11373
718-592-6593

A Center for the Awareness of
Pattern
P.O. Box 407
Freeport, ME 04032
207-865-3396

Clear Mountain Zen Center
605 Peninsula Boulevard
Hempstead, NY 11550
516-564-9808

Dai Bosatsu Zendo
HRC 1 Box 171
Livingston Manor, NY 12758
845-439-4566

Zen Mountain Monastery
P.O. Box 197TR
Mount Tremper, NY 12457
914-688-2228

New Haven Zen Center
193 Mansfield Street
New Haven, CT 06511
203-787-0912

Chogye International Zen
    Center
400 East 14th Street, #2E
New York, NY 10009
212-353-0461

Community of Mindfulness
New York, NY 10024
212-501-2652

First Zen Institute of America
113 East 30th Street
New York, NY 10016
212-686-2520

New York Zendo Shobo-ji
223 East 67th Street
New York, NY 10021
212-861-3333

Soho Zendo
464 West Broadway
New York, NY 10012
212-460-9289

Village Zendo
Greenwich Village
New York, NY 10003
212-340-4656

Zen Studies Society
223 East 67th Street
New York, NY 10021
212-861-3333

Plum Tree Zendo
214 Monroe Street
Philadelphia, PA 19147
215-625-2601

Rochester Zen Center
7 Arnold Park
Rochester, NY 14607
716-473-9180

Empty Hand Zendo
624 Milton Road
Rye, NY 10580
914-921-3327

Vermont Zen Center
14 Thomas Road
Shelburne, VT 05482
802-985-9746

Morgan Bay Zendo
P.O. Box 188
Surry, ME 04684
207-374-9963

Zen Center of Syracuse
266 West Seneca Turnpike
Syracuse, NY 13207
315-492-9773

SOUTHEAST

Atlanta Soto Zen Center
1404 McLendon Avenue N.E.
Atlanta, GA 30307
404-659-4749

Baltimore Zendo, Shorin-ji
P.O. Box 3514
Baltimore, MD 21214
410-254-5128

Chapel Hill Zen Center
P.O. Box 16302
Chapel Hill, NC 27516
919-967-0861

Charlotte Zen Meditation
Society
P.O. Box 32512
Charlotte, NC 28232
704-523-7373

Sai Sho An Zen Group
Delaplane, VA 20144
540-592-3701

Green Mountain Zen Center
5014 Sunset Bluff Drive S.E.
Huntsville, AL 35803
256-882-0513

International Zen Institute of
Florida
3860 Crawford Avenue
Miami, FL 33133
305-448-8969

New Orleans Zen Temple
748 Camp Street
New Orleans, LA 70130
504-523-1213

Squirrel Mountain Zendo
283 Quartz Hill Road
Pittsboro, NC 27312
919-542-1249

Stone Mountain Zendo
2702 Avenel Avenue S.W.
Roanoke, VA 24015
703-345-8209

Cypress Tree Zen Group
P.O. Box 247
Tallahassee, FL 32302
850-877-4663

MIDWEST

Zen Buddhist Temple
1214 Packard Road
Ann Arbor, MI 48104
734-761-6520

Zen Buddhist Temple
1710 West Cornelia
Chicago, IL 60657
773-528-8685

Dharma Center of Cincinnati
P.O. Box 23307
Cincinnati, OH 45223
513-281-6453

Northwest Chicago Zen Group
Des Plaines, IL 60016
847-298-8472

Zen Buddhist Temple—Chicago
608 Dempster Street
Evanston, IL 60212
847-272-2070

Detroit Zen Center
11464 Mitchell Street
Hamtramck, MI 48212
313-366-7738

Zen Center of Hot Springs
P.O. Box 1260
Hot Springs, AR 71902
501-767-6096

Indianapolis Zen Center
5335 N. Tacoma Avenue, #4
Indianapolis, IN 46244
317-274-6879

Iowa City Zen Center
226 South Johnson Street, #2A
Iowa City, IA 52240
319-354-1997

Kearney Zendo
3715 Avenue F
Kearney, NE 68847
308-236-5650

Madison Zen Center
1820 Jefferson Street
Madison, WI 53711
608-255-4488

Milwaukee Zen Center
2825 North Stowell Avenue
Milwaukee, WI 53211
414-963-0526

Minnesota Zen Meditation
    Center
3343 East Calhoun Parkway
Minneapolis, MN 55408
612-822 5313

Nebraska Zen Center
3625 Lafayette Avenue
Omaha, NE 68131
402-551-9035

Clouds in Water Zen Center
308 Prince Street, #120
St. Paul, MN 55101
651-222-6968

WEST

Hidden Mountain Zen Center
216 Ninth Street N.W.
Albuquerque, NM 87102
505-248-0649

Anchorage Zen Community
2401 Susitna
Anchorage, AK 99517
907-566-0143

Berkeley Zen Center
1931 Russell Street
Berkeley, CA 94703
510-845-2403

Community of Mindful Living
P.O. Box 7355
Berkeley, CA 94707
510-527-3751

Empty Gate Zen Center
2200 Parker Street
Berkeley, CA 94704
510-845-8565

Sixth Patriarch Zen Center
2584 Martin Luther King Jr. Way
Berkeley, CA 94704
510-486-1762

Tassajara Zen Mountain Center
39171 Tassajara Road
Carmel Valley, CA 93924
415-863-3136

Zen Community of Oregon
P.O. Box 7
Corbett, OR 97019
503-282-7879

Newport Mesa Zen Center
711 West 17th Street A8
Costa Mesa, CA 92627
714-722-7818

Maria Kannon Zen Center
P.O. Box 140662
Dallas, TX 75214
214-361-1066

Three Treasures Zen
   Community
P.O. Box 754
Del Mar, CA 92014
760-745-4249

Denver Zen Center
3101 West 31st Avenue
Denver, CO 80211
303-455-1500

Honolulu Diamond Sangha
Palolo Zen Center
2747 Walamao Road
Honolulu, HI 96816
808-735-1347

Houston Zen Community
P.O. Box 54229
Houston, TX 77254
713-869-6266

Zen Center of Hawai'i
P.O. Box 2066
Kamuela, HI 96743
808-885-6109

Mojave Desert Zen Center
5115 S. Industrial Road, 903
Las Vegas, NV 89118
702-293-4222

California Buddhist University
3165 Minnesota Street
Los Angeles, CA 90031
213-628-3449

International Buddhist
    Meditation Center
928 South New Hampshire
    Avenue
Los Angeles, CA 90006
213-384-0850

Rinzai-ji Zen Center
2505 Cimarron Street
Los Angeles, CA 90018
213-732-2263

Zen Center of Los Angeles
923 South Normandie Avenue
Los Angeles, CA 90006
213-387-2351

Desert Zen Center
10989 Buena Vista
Lucerne Valley, CA 92356
760-248-7082

Open Way Sangha
P.O. Box 7281
Missoula, MT 59807
406-549-9005, ext. 3

Mount Baldy Zen Center
P.O. Box 429
Mount Baldy, CA 91759
909-985-6410

Zen Mountain Center
P.O. Box 43
Mountain Center, CA 92561
909-659-5272

Dharma Rain Zen Center
2539 Southeast Madison
Portland, OR 97214
503-239-4846

Kanzeon Zen Center
1280 East South Temple
Salt Lake City, UT 84102
801-328-8414

Shaolin Chi Mantis
P.O. Box 58547
Salt Lake City, UT 84158
801-595-1123

Zen Center of San Diego
2047 Felspar Street
San Diego, CA 92109
619-273-3444

Gay Buddhist Fellowship
2261 Market Street, no. 422
San Francisco, CA 94114
415-974-9878

Harbor Sangha
1032 Irving Street
P.O. Box 330
San Francisco, CA 94122
415-241-8807

San Francisco Zen Center
300 Page Street
San Francisco, CA 94102
415-863-3136

Santa Barbara Buddhist Priory
1115 Tunnel Road
Santa Barbara, CA 93015
805-898-0848

Santa Cruz Zen Center
113 School Street
Santa Cruz, CA 95060
408-457-0206

Upaya
1404 Cerro Gordo Road
Santa Fe, NM 87501
505-986-8518

Santa Monica Zen Center
1001A Colorado Avenue
Santa Monica, CA 90401
310-572-9070

California Diamond Sangha
P.O. Box 2972
Santa Rosa, CA 95405
707-793-2138

Sonoma Mountain Zen Center
6367 Sonoma Mountain Road
Santa Rosa, CA 95404
707-545-8105

Green Gulch Farm
1601 Shoreline Highway
Sausalito, CA 94965
415-383-3134

Dharma Sound Zen Center
P.O. Box 31003
Seattle, WA 98103
206-783-8484

Three Treasures Sangha
P.O. Box 12542
Seattle, WA 98111
206-322-2447

Stone Creek Zendo
P.O. Box 1053
Sebastopol, CA 95473
707-829-9808

Hakuun-ji Zen Center
1448 East Cedar Street
Tempe, AZ 85281
480-894-6353

Zen Desert Sangha
P.O. Box 44122
Tucson, AZ 85733
520-620-6347

Canada

Association Zen de Montréal
982 Gilford East
Montreal, Quebec,
Canada H2J 1P4
514-523-1543

Centre Zen de la Main
30 rue Vallières
Montreal, Quebec,
Canada H2W 1C2
514-842-3648

Montreal Zen Center
824 Park Stanley
Montreal, Quebec,
Canada H2C 1A2
514-388-4518

White Wind Zen Community
240 Daly Avenue
Ottawa, Ontario,
Canada K1N 6G2
613-562-1568

Toronto Zen Center
33 High Park Gardens
Toronto, Ontario,
Canada M6R 1S8
416-766-3400

Zen Buddhist Temple
297 College Street
Toronto, Ontario,
Canada M6C 2M1
416-658-0137

Zen Center of Vancouver
4269 Brant Street
Vancouver, British Columbia,
Canada V5N 3K4
604-879-0229

Zen Center of Vancouver
4956 Cordova Bay Road
Victoria, British Columbia,
Canada V8Y 2K1
250-658-5033

France

Association Zen Internationale
175 rue Tolbiac
75013 Paris, France
33-1-53-80-19-19

Germany

Zen Zentrum Mumon-kai
Frohnauer Str. 148
13465 Berlin, Germany
49-30-401-30-69

Zen-Institut-Deutschland
Striehweg 32
72820 Sonnenbühl, Germany
49-7128-784

Netherlands

Kanzeon Zen Centre
Krayenhoffstraat 151
1018 RG Amsterdam, The
  Netherlands
31-20-627-6493

United Kingdom

The Buddhist Society
58 Eccleston Square
London SW1P 1PH, England
44-171-834-5858

London Fo Kuang Temple
84 Margaret Street
London W1N 7HD, England
44-171-636-8394

OTHER RESOURCES

....

JOURNALS

Tricycle: The Buddhist Review
92 Vandam Street
New York, NY 10013
212-645-1143
email: editorial@tricycle.com
Web:http://www.tricycle.com

Turning Wheel
Buddhist Peace Fellowship
P.O. Box 4650
Berkeley, CA 94704
510-655-6169
email: bpf@bpf.org
Web: http://www.bpf.org

SELECTED WEBSITES

Association Zen Internationale, Paris
Web: http://www.zen-azi.org/

Buddhist Information Service of New York
Web: http://www.infinite.org/bodhiline

Buddhist InfoWeb (DharmaNet)
Web: http://www.dharmanet.org/infowebt.html

Buddhist Peace Fellowship
email: bpf@bpf.org
Web: http://www.bpf.org

Buddhist Studies WWW Virtual Library
Web: http://www.ciolek.com/WWWVL-Buddhism.html
Web: http://www.ciolek.com/WWWVL-Zen.html

Community of Mindful Living (Thich Nhat Hanh)
Web: http://www.parallax.org

Dai Bosatsu Zendo Kongo-Ji
Web: http://www.daibosatsu.org

Providence Zen Center
email: kwanumzen@compuserve.com
Web: http://www.kwanumzen.com

San Francisco Zen Center
Beginner's Mind Temple
Green Gulch Farm
Tassajara Zen Mountain Center
Web: http://www.bodhi.sfzc.com

Zen Center of Los Angeles
Web: http://www.zencenter.org

Zen Mountain Center
email: zmc@primenet.com
Web: http://www.zmc.org

Zen Mountain Monastery
email: zmmtrain@zen-mtn.org.
Web: http://www.zen-mtn.org

Zen Peacemaker Order
email: info@peacemakeroffice.com
Web: http://www.peacemakercommunity.org

at Upaya Peace Institute
email: upaya@upaya.org
Web: http://www.upaya.org

Selected Glossary of Terms

in Zen Buddhism

Anatman (Sanskrit) "no self," the nonexistence of a permanent, unchanging soul

Atman (Sanskrit) a permanent, unchanging soul

Avalokiteshvara (Sanskrit) the embodiment of compassion

beginner's mind the phrase used by Shunryu Suzuki to describe the ability to meet every experience with the innocence of first inquiry

bhikkhu (Sanskrit) a member of the Buddha's *sangha;* a *monk*

Bodhidharma the legendary Indian master believed to have arrived in China in 520 C.E. and who is recognized as the First Ancestor, or Patriarch, of *Ch'an/Zen*

bodhisattva (Sanskrit) a being who seeks enlightenment in order to end the suffering and bring about the enlightenment of all other beings

Bodhisattva Precepts Sixteen precepts that consist of the *Three Treasures,* the *Three Pure Precepts,* and the *Ten Grave Precepts*

Brahman/Brahmin (Sanskrit) the strong priestly class who were the interpreters between gods and the people during the *Buddha's* time

buddha (Sanskrit) "awakened," "enlightened"

Buddha the historical figure, probably born during the sixth century B.C.E. (563–483 B.C.E.?) into the Shakya clan, in what is now Nepal, who was given the name *Siddhartha Gautama*; also known as *Shakyamuni Buddha* ("the Buddha of the Shakya clan")

Buddha-charita (Sanskrit) "Life of the Buddha"; Ashvaghosha's first-century epic poem

Buddha hall a hall where services are held

Buddha-mind or Buddha-nature the mind of *not knowing,* of oneness, of complete intimacy with the interrelatedness and interpenetration of all things

Burmese position the meditation posture in which legs are simply folded in front of the body

Ch'an the Chinese Buddhist sect believed founded in the sixth century by the legendary Indian master *Bodhidharma,* who is honored as the First Ancestor of *Ch'an,* which became *Zen* in Japan

Chogye the order founded in Korea by Son master Chinul in the late twelfth century

circumambulation walking in a circle around a *Buddha* image on an altar or in a circle, representing reverence for the unity of all things

clackers wooden sounders used to mark intervals in services

conditional arising the interconnection and interdependence of all things, so that anything arising affects everything else; also called codependent origination

cosmic mudra the hand position *(dhyani mudra)* in which the active hand, palm up, cradles the passive hand, and the thumbs meet in front of the navel, forming an oval

dana (Sanskrit) "generosity"; individual donations that may be given to the teacher or to a teacher's discretionary fund in support of the teachings

Deer Park   the park in Benares (Sarnath) where the *Buddha* gave his first sermon: the *Four Noble Truths*

Dhammapada   an early collection of the *Buddha*'s sayings in verse

Dharma (Sanskrit)   Buddhist teachings or doctrine; *dharma* also means "all elements, all things, the law, the truth"

Dharma combat   a teaching exchange between a teacher and a student in which the teacher's introductory remarks are used as seeds for the encounter

Dharma hall   the hall where a *Dharma talk* is given

Dharma holder   a senior student entrusted with teaching responsibilities, under the guidance of his or her *sensei*

Dharma talk   a teacher's discourse exploring various aspects of *Zen* teachings and practice

Dharmakaya (Sanskrit, "the body of the teachings")   the unity of the *Buddha*'s existence with all things

dhyana (Sanskrit)   "meditative absorption"

Dogen (1200–1253)   the Japanese master who brought the *Soto* tradition from China to Japan in the early thirteenth century

dokusan (Japanese)   a private interview with a teacher held during a meditation period

dukkha   the Pali term describing the quality of dissatisfaction, discomfort, and impatience that is part of everyday life; often translated as "suffering"

Eightfold Path   the *Buddha*'s teachings on the way to end *dukkha* through *Right Action, Right Speech, Right Livelihood, Right Thought, Right View, Right Mindfulness, Right Concentration,* and *Right Effort*

Eisai (1141–1215)   the Japanese master of the Oryo lineage who, in the late twelfth century, founded the first *Rinzai* (Chinese *Lin-chi*) monastery in Japan

emptiness (in Japanese, *ku,* "sky" or "void"), the stripping away of all definitions and notions of each and every thing; see also *shunyata*

engaged Buddhism social action in the broadest sense of taking care of everything in your life as well as confronting the ills of society

enlightenment seeing into one's true nature and experiencing oneness with all things; being free of the delusion of a separate self; see also *satori* and *kensho*

First Council a gathering of five hundred senior disciples called by senior disciple Mahakashyapa approximately one month after the *Buddha*'s death. The *Buddha*'s attendant, Ananda, recited all the *Dharma* teachings, and another disciple, Upali, recited the *Vinaya.* These recitations were accepted by the council as the *Buddha*'s authentic teachings and are the foundation of the teachings that have come down as the *Pali canon,* especially in the *Theravada* tradition.

First Noble Truth *dukkha* is the intrinsic nature of existence

Four Noble Truths the *Buddha*'s fundamental teaching—that *dukkha* is the intrinsic nature of existence; that it has a cause; that it can be ended; that the method for ending *dukkha* is the *Eightfold Path*

Fourth Noble Truth the way to end *dukkha* is through the *Eightfold Path*

gassho (Japanese) a bow with the palms together in front of the chest

gatha (Sanskrit) a verse or song, commonly chanted during a ritual

haiku the Japanese sixteen-syllable poetry form that expresses the nonduality of *Zen*

hako (Japanese) a box for incense burned during services

half lotus posture *(hankafuza)*   the cross-legged meditation position in which the right foot, sole up, is placed on the left thigh, and the left leg is folded in front of the body, with the left foot on the floor

han (Japanese)   a wooden board that is hit with a wood striker to summon people to sitting periods

hankafuza (Japanese)   the half lotus meditation posture

hara (Japanese)   the area about an inch below the navel that in *Zen* is considered the center of the body

Hui-neng (Chinese; E'no in Japanese)   an illiterate woodcutter who became the Sixth Ch'an Ancestor and greatly affected the shape of *Ch'an* Buddhism

ikebana   Japanese flower design, within the framework of *Zen*

isshu (Japanese)   a hand position for walking meditation in which a fist is made with the right (or left) hand, enclosing the thumb, and the top of the fist is covered with the left (or right) palm. Elbows are held at right angles and away from the body. In *isshu* both hands are turned downward with the thumbs next to the chest. See also *shashu*.

jukai (Japanese)   the ceremony in which *Zen* disciples are initiated into Buddhism by committing themselves to the *Three Treasures,* the precepts, and the Four Vows

karma (Sanskrit)   "action" or "deed," as well as the fruit of action; cause and effect

kekkafuza (Japanese)   the full lotus meditation posture

kensho (Japanese)   "enlightenment"; usually refers to the individual's initial self-realization

kesa (Japanese)   the bib derived from and symbolic of the patchwork shawl originally worn by Buddhist *monks;* today worn by *monks* and priests during *sesshin* and for ceremonial occasions; see also *rakusu*

kinhin (Japanese)   walking meditation done by a group in a line or circle

koan (Japanese)   a paradoxical phrase or story that transcends logic; most frequently used by teachers in the *Rinzai* tradition

ku   a Japanese word for "emptiness" that also means "sky" or "void"; skylike or empty mind is *ku;* see also *shunyata*

Kwan Um school   founded by contemporary Korean Chogye master Seung Sahn, with many temples in the West

kyosaku (Japanese)   a flattened "wake-up" stick about the size of a yardstick, symbolic of the sword of *Manjushri,* used to encourage and stimulate people who have become sleepy during long meditation periods

Lin-chi (Chinese; Japanese, Rinzai)   major *Ch'an* sect founded in the mid-ninth century by Lin-chi

lotus posture *(kekkafuza)*   the most stable and traditional cross-legged meditation position, in which the right foot, sole up, is placed on the left thigh, and the left foot, sole up, is placed on the right thigh

Mahasangha (Sanskrit)   "Great Sangha"; a sect that split off after the *Second Council* and probably was a forerunner of *Mahayana* and therefore *Zen* Buddhism

Mahayana (Sanskrit)   the "Great Vehicle" tradition, which encompasses both *Zen* and Tibetan Buddhism and stresses seeking enlightenment for all beings

Manjushri (Sanskrit)   the embodiment of Wisdom; the image of Buddha-consciousness that holds a sword to cut off delusions

Mara (Sanskrit)   embodiment of death or murder, often used as the manifestation of our minds

Middle Way   the balance of mind and body in daily life, advocated by the *Buddha*

monk   a renunciant who may live in a monastery; a *bhikkhu*

monkey mind   a mind that is "running around and swinging from tree to tree"

mu (Japanese; Chinese *Wu*)   "no," "nothing," "not"; Joshu's (Chaochou's) enigmatic response in the classic koan when asked if a dog has Buddha-nature

nirvana (Sanskrit)   literally, "blown out"—the state of being where there is no grasping or desire for things to be different than they are

no self (**Anatman**)   the absence of a separate, independent, eternal self or soul

nonduality   having no separate self, not seeing things as different from oneself

not knowing   having dropped away the separation between the knower and the known; there is nothing to know because you are it

ordination   the ceremonial induction into a specific Zen lineage as a *monk* or nun

oryoki (Japanese)   ceremonially taken meals

Oxherding Pictures   ten inspirational visual expressions of Zen Buddhism created in China in the twelfth century

Pali canon   the body of teachings of the *Buddha* affirmed immediately after his death, transmitted orally for several hundred years, then recorded in Pali, a language predating and similar to Sanskrit; the central documents in *Theravada* Buddhism

Parinirvana (Sanskrit)   the Buddha's "extinction," or final release from *samsara,* at Kushinagara (in modern Uttar Pradesh)

Prajna Paramita (Sanskrit)   the "wisdom that reaches the other shore"—literature, especially *The Heart Sutra* and *The Diamond Sutra,* that teaches that everything is empty

prostration a deep bow in which one begins standing, then kneels in the *seiza* position, *gasshos*, and leans forward, extending the hands— palms upward—while simultaneously touching the forehead to the floor and raising the palms a few inches above the head

rakusu (Japanese) the rectangular patchwork bib symbolizing the *Buddha*'s robes, worn by initiates (lay and monastic) who have taken formal Buddhist vows; see also *kesa*

Right Action acting in a way that causes no harm, especially avoiding killing or harming other beings, sexual misconduct, and abusing intoxicants

Right Concentration meditation, taking the time to "step into oneself" and really be aware of the workings of the mind and body, to allow oneself to let go and just be in great emptiness

Right Effort continually striving for mindfulness, especially in meditation

Right Livelihood earning one's living according to the teachings of the Buddha

Right Mindfulness awareness during everything one does in life

Right Speech speaking in a way that causes no harm

Right Thought directing one's thoughts toward getting off the wheel of suffering and grasping

Right View understanding the world so that one can experience life with wisdom and compassion

Rinzai (Chinese, Lin-chi) the *Zen* tradition in which there is a strong impulse to koan study and a vigorous and active style within the monasteries

roshi (Japanese) literally, "old teacher"—a title given in some lineages as an ultimate empowerment, usually after many years of teaching

sadhu (Sanskrit)   a wandering ascetic on a spiritual path

samadhi (Sanskrit)   concentration meditation practice; single-pointed focus

samsara (Sanskrit)   day-to-day life

samu (Japanese)   the work period during a *sesshin* or as part of monastic life

sangha (Sanskrit)   spiritual community—originally a particular group of *monks* living under quite specific guidelines (Sangha), but now expanded to include nuns, novitiates, lay practitioners, and sometimes all who follow a spiritual path

satori (Japanese)   "enlightenment"; usually refers to the experience of the *Buddha* or the *Zen* Ancestors

Second Council   a gathering of senior *monks*, called about a hundred years after the *Buddha's* death, that reaffirmed the *Vinaya*

Second Noble Truth   the cause of *dukkha* is grasping, greed, and the desire for things to be different from what they are

seiza   the traditional Japanese kneeling position for meditation, with the knees apart, then sitting back on the heels, keeping the spine erect

seiza bench   a three-piece meditation bench with a slanted plank about 8 inches wide and 12 inches long and two side planks about 8 inches high

sensei (Japanese)   "teacher"; the title given a *Zen* teacher that implies that the teacher has received recognition from his or her own teacher and can independently carry out all teaching activities

sesshin (Japanese)   a regularly scheduled period of intensive practice, usually lasting in the West for six days

Shakyamuni (Sanskrit)   the "sage of the Shakya clan"; the historical Buddha

shashu (Japanese)   a hand position for walking meditation in which

·

a fist is made with the right (or left) hand, enclosing the thumb, and the top of the fist is covered with the left (or right) palm. Elbows are held at right angles and away from the body. In *shashu* both hands are against the chest, with thumbs upward. See also *isshu.*

shunyata (Japanese) "emptiness," in the central teaching that everything is impermanent and lacks a self-nature

shikantaza (Japanese) literally "nothing but precise sitting"; the purest form of *zazen*

Siddhartha Gautama the given name of the historical *Buddha*

sila (Sanskrit) the term used primarily in *Theravada* Buddhism for "morality," especially *Right Speech, Right Action,* and *Right Livelihood*

skandha (Sanskrit) one of the five aggregates of one's being: form, sensation, perception, mental formations, and consciousness

Son Korea's version of *Ch'an* or *Zen*

Soto (Japanese; Chinese, Ts'ao-tung) the *Zen* tradition founded by Tung-shan and his student Ts'ao-shan, in which there is a great reverence for form and an emphasis on silent illumination or *shikantaza,* just sitting

sutra (Sanskrit) literally "thread"; a Buddhist discourse

Tathagata (Sanskrit) "everythingness," "suchness"; the "thus-come" one, when referring to the *Buddha*

Ten Grave Precepts not killing; not stealing; not misusing sex; not telling lies; not using intoxicants; not talking about others' errors and faults; not elevating oneself and blaming others; not being stingy; not being angry; and not speaking ill of the *Three Treasures*

Theravada the "teachings of the elders," the oldest Buddhist tradition, which exists in the West primarily as Vipassana, or Insight Meditation, and stresses the enlightenment of the individual. Also disparagingly called Hinayana ("Lesser Vehicle") by early *Mahayana* Buddhists.

Thien   Vietnam's version of *Ch'an* or *Zen*

Third Noble Truth   there is an end to the cycle of wanting something, being dissatisfied, wishing things were different, and constantly creating *dukkha* within oneself

Three Pure Precepts   not doing evil; doing good; doing good for others

Three Treasures   Be one with the *Buddha* / Be one with the *Dharma* / Be one with the *Sangha*. Also called the Triple Jewel.

tokudo (Japanese)   "ordination," after which the person wears priestly robes and is authorized to officiate at services and rituals

Ts'ao tung (Chinese, Japanese, Soto)   major *Ch'an* sect founded in the mid-ninth century by Ts'ao-shan and Tung-shan

Vinaya (Sanskrit)   the codified rules of conduct for *monks* established in the first *sangha*

vipassana (Sanskrit)   insight meditation. See also *Theravada*

zabuton (Japanese)   a mat, about one and a half by three feet, used in meditation, often under a *zafu*

zafu (Japanese)   a small, often round cushion used in meditation

zazen (Japanese)   literally, "seated mind"; meditation

Zen   from the Sanskrit *dhyana* ("meditative absorption"), which was transliterated into *ch'an* in Chinese, then into *zenna,* or *Zen,* in Japanese

Zen Peacemaker Order   founded by Bernie and Jishu Glassman to link people who are engaged in social action and *Zen* Buddhism

zendo (Japanese)   a hall where *zazen* is formally practiced

Index

About the Author

After several decades in the corporate world, during which she became the first woman to head a college publishing company, JEAN SMITH decided to devote her time to writing, traveling, and being. She divides her time between New York City and a 120-year-old house in the Adirondack Mountains, thoroughly enjoying both with her companion bodhisattva, an Affenpinscher named Ani Metta. Her writing interests and current projects include Buddhism, humanities, and fiction set in the Himalayas. And in her spare time, she sits and watches the river go by.

OTHER BELL TOWER BOOKS

....

Books that nourish the soul, illuminate the mind,
and speak directly to the heart

Valeria Alfeyeva
PILGRIMAGE TO DZHVARI
....
A Woman's Journey of Spiritual Awakening
An unforgettable introduction to the riches of the Eastern Orthodox
mystical tradition. A modern *Way of a Pilgrim.*
0-517-88389-9 • *Softcover*

Rob Baker
PLANNING MEMORIAL CELEBRATIONS
....
A Sourcebook
A one-stop handbook for a situation more and more of us are facing as
we grow older. • 0-609-80404-9 • *Softcover*

Thomas Berry
THE GREAT WORK
....
Our Way into the Future
The author of *The Dream of the Earth* teaches us how to move from a
human-centered view of the world to one focused on the earth and all
its inhabitants. • 0-609-60525-9 • *Hardcover*

Cynthia Bourgeault
LOVE IS STRONGER THAN DEATH
....
The Mystical Union of Two Souls
Both the story of the incandescent love between two hermits and a
guidebook for those called to this path of soulwork.
0-609-60473-2 • *Hardcover*

Madeline Bruser

THE ART OF PRACTICING

Making Music from the Heart

A classic work on how to practice music that combines meditative prin
ciples with information on body mechanics and medicine.
0 609 80177-5 • *Softcover*

Melody Ermachild Chavis

ALTARS IN THE STREET

A Courageous Memoir of Community and Spiritual Awakening
A deeply moving account that captures the essence of human struggles
and resourcefulness. • 0-609-80196-1 • *Softcover*

David A. Cooper

ENTERING THE SACRED MOUNTAIN

Exploring the Mystical Practices of Judaism, Buddhism, and Sufism
An inspiring chronicle of one man's search for truth.
0-517-88464-x • *Softcover*

Marc David

NOURISHING WISDOM

A Mind/Body Approach to Nutrition and Well-Being
A book that advocates awareness in eating. • 0-517-88129-2 • *Softcover*

Kat Duff

THE ALCHEMY OF ILLNESS

A luminous inquiry into the function and purpose of illness.
0-517-88097-0 • *Softcover*

Joan Furman, MSN, RN, and David McNabb

THE DYING TIME

Practical Wisdom for the Dying and Their Caregivers
A comprehensive guide, filled with physical, emotional, and spiritual
advice. • 0-609-80003-5 • *Softcover*

Bernard Glassman

BEARING WITNESS

A Zen Master's Lessons in Making Peace
How Glassman started the Zen Peacemaker Order and what each of us
can do to make peace in our hearts and in the world.
0-609-80391-3 • *Softcover*

Bernard Glassman and Rick Fields
INSTRUCTIONS TO THE COOK
A Zen Master's Lessons in Living a Life That Matters

A distillation of Zen wisdom that can be used equally well as a manual on business or spiritual practice, cooking or life.
0-517-88829-7 • *Softcover*

Burghild Nina Holzer
A WALK BETWEEN HEAVEN AND EARTH
A Personal Journal on Writing and the Creative Process

How keeping a journal focuses and expands our awareness of ourselves and everything that touches our lives. • 0-517-88096-2 • *Softcover*

Greg Johanson and Ron Kurtz
GRACE UNFOLDING
Psychotherapy in the Spirit of the Tao-te ching

The interaction of client and therapist illuminated through the gentle power and wisdom of Lao Tsu's ancient classic.
0-517-88130-6 • *Softcover*

Selected by Marcia and Jack Kelly
ONE HUNDRED GRACES
Mealtime Blessings

A collection of graces from many traditions, inscribed in calligraphy reminiscent of the manuscripts of medieval Europe.
0-517-58567-7 • *Hardcover* / 0-609-80093-0 • *Softcover*

Jack and Marcia Kelly
SANCTUARIES
A Guide to Lodgings in Monasteries, Abbeys, and Retreats of the United States

For those in search of renewal and a little peace; described by the *New York Times* as "the Michelin Guide of the retreat set."
0-517-88517-4 • *Softcover*

Marcia and Jack Kelly
THE WHOLE HEAVEN CATALOG
A Resource Guide to Products, Services, Arts, Crafts, and Festivals of Religious, Spiritual, and Cooperative Communities

All the things that monks and nuns do to support their habits!
0-609-80120-1 • *Softcover*

Barbara Lachman
THE JOURNAL OF HILDEGARD OF BINGEN
A year in the life of the twelfth-century German saint—the diary she never had the time to write herself. • 0-517-88390-2 • *Softcover*

Stephen Levine
A YEAR TO LIVE
How to Live This Year as if It Were Your Last
Using the consciousness of our mortality to enter into a new and vibrant relationship with life. • 0-609-80194-5 • *Softcover*

Gunilla Norris
BEING HOME
A Book of Meditations
An exquisite modern book of hours, a celebration of mindfulness in everyday activities. • 0-517-58159-0 • *Hardcover*

Marcia Prager
THE PATH OF BLESSING
Experiencing the Energy and Abundance of the Divine
How to use the traditional Jewish practice of calling down a blessing on each action as a profound path of spiritual growth.
0-609-80393-X • *Softcover*

Saki Santorelli
HEAL THYSELF
Lessons on Mindfulness in Medicine
An invitation to patients and health care professionals to bring mindfulness into the crucible of the healing relationship. • 0-609-60385-X • *Hardcover*

Rabbi Rami M. Shapiro
MINYAN
Ten Principles for Living a Life of Integrity
A primer for those interested to know what Judaism has to offer the spiritually hungry. • 0-609-80055-8 • *Softcover*

Rabbi Rami M. Shapiro
WISDOM OF THE JEWISH SAGES
A Modern Reading of Pirke Avot
A third-century treasury of maxims on justice, integrity, and virtue—Judaism's principal ethical scripture. • 0-517-79966-9 • *Hardcover*

James Thornton
A FIELD GUIDE TO THE SOUL

A Down-to-Earth Handbook of Spiritual Practice

A manual for coming into harmony and communion with the earth.
0-609-60368-X • *Hardcover*

Joan Tollifson
BARE-BONES MEDITATION

Waking Up from the Story of My Life

An unvarnished, exhilarating account of one woman's struggle to make sense of her life. • 0-517-88792-4 • *Softcover*

Michael Toms and Justine Willis Toms
TRUE WORK

Doing What You Love and Loving What You Do

Wisdom for the workplace from the husband-and-wife team of NPR's weekly radio program New Dimensions. • 0-609-80212-7 • *Softcover*

BUDDHA LAUGHING

A Tricycle *Book of Cartoons*

A marvelous opportunity for self-reflection for those who tend to take themselves too seriously. • 0-609-80409-X • *Softcover*

Ed. Richard Whelan
SELF-RELIANCE

The Wisdom of Ralph Waldo Emerson as Inspiration for Daily Living

A distillation of Emerson's spiritual writings for contemporary readers.
0-517-58512-X • *Softcover*

 Bell Tower books are for sale at your local bookstore or you may call Random House at 1-800-793-BOOK to order with a credit card.